ELIZABETHAN HANDWRITING

1500–1650

A MANUAL

ELIZABETHAN
HANDWRITING
1500–1650
A MANUAL

Giles E. Dawson   *Laetitia Kennedy-Skipton*

OF THE FOLGER SHAKESPEARE LIBRARY

W · W · NORTON & COMPANY · INC ·

NEW YORK

PREFACE

❁

The brief success of William Henry Ireland's crude Shakespeare forgeries, about 1800, shows how little attention had up to that time been paid to the handwriting of the sixteenth century. Fifty years later he would have had to do a much better job and probably could have. By then there were learned experts in English paleography at the British Museum, the Public Record Office, and elsewhere.

But it was not until well into our own century that anybody gave much thought to the needs of students who had to work with the historical and literary documents of the time of Shakespeare and Queen Elizabeth. In 1925 Miss M. St. Clair Byrne published an article (see the Reading List) in which she says that "Elizabethan palaeography is something which has to be learnt," provides an annotated alphabet, and reproduces a specimen of Elizabethan writing. She deplores the fact that little attention had been paid to what she calls "the ordinary English current hand used by practically everybody for ordinary purposes until about the end of the [seventeenth] century"—by which she meant what was in its own day called the secretary hand. R. B. McKerrow in 1927 supplemented Miss Byrne's article by another one devoted to the capital letters in the secretary hand. In 1930 appeared S. A. Tannenbaum's much more ambitious treatise, which, though helpful, is neither well planned nor altogether reliable.

That is almost the whole story. While a score of books and pamphlets have described, discussed, illustrated, and extolled the italic hand and Charles Johnson and Hilary Jenkinson have produced a monumental exposition of the court hands, the secretary hand, the hand of literature, correspondence, and business, has remained largely neglected. Its origins have not been much investigated, and no attempt has hitherto been made to produce a practical handbook. The student of English history or English literature who has faced the need to read Elizabethan manuscripts has not usually known where to turn for the kind of help he needed. Such help the present manual is designed in some degree to provide.

Our own experience has persuaded us that the only pathway to facility in the secretary hand is through the reading of many and varied examples. We have therefore chosen the specimens in this book with a primary view to providing variety of hands and, after that, variety of form and matter.

All of the manuscripts reproduced are in the collections of the Folger Shakespeare Library. We are indebted to the trustees of the Library and to its director, Louis B. Wright, for the opportunity to make this use of the material; to the latter for advice and encouragement; to Horace Groves, chief of the photographic department, for the exercise of his skill and judgment in making fifty-four difficult photographs of high quality.

THE FOLGER SHAKESPEARE LIBRARY

GILES E. DAWSON
LAETITIA KENNEDY-SKIPTON

CONTENTS

Preface   v

INTRODUCTION

1. The Survival of Manuscripts   3
2. The Handwriting of the Tudor and Stuart Age   7
3. Historical Development   10
4. The Mechanics of Writing   13
    Some Letters of the Secretary Hand · Spelling · Punctuation ·
    Abbreviation and Contraction
5. Editorial Principles   22
6. Methods of Study   24

PLATES AND TRANSCRIPTS

1A Robert Mannyng of Brunne, an extract from *Handlyng Synne*
     [ca. 1400]   28

1B An extract from *Mind, Will, and Understanding*, a morality play
     [ca. 1460]   28

2A J. de Beau Chesne and J. Baildon, a woodcut engraving from *A Booke
     Containing Divers Sortes of Hands* [1571]   30

2B J. de Beau Chesne and J. Baildon, *A New Booke Containing All Sorts
     of Hands* [1611]   30

3   A deed conveying land, 1501   32

4   Henry VIII, warrant, 1525   34

5   Henry Fitzalan, earl of Arundel, an order to the Office of Tents and
     Revels, 1549   36

6   Receipt for armor [1554]   38

7   Sir William Cavendish, letter to Sir Humphrey Bradborne and
     Thomas Babington [ca. 1555]   40

8   Prologue to *July and Julian* (anonymous school play) [ca. 1560]   42

9   Sir George Pierrepoint, autograph letter to Elizabeth, Lady St. Loe,
     1561   44

10 James Crompe, letter to Elizabeth, Lady St. Loe [ca. 1565]   46

11 Ralph Adderley, letter to Sir Nicholas Bagnal, 1567   48

12 Privy Council, letter probably to the lieutenant of Dover Castle, 1572   50

13 Walter Devereux, earl of Essex, letter to George Talbot, earl of Shrewsbury, 1573 52

14 Indenture of release, 1576 54

15 A Post-mortem inventory of the goods of John Edolf, 1576 56

16 Richard Broughton, autograph letter to Richard Bagot [1577] 58

17 John Kay, a lesson for landbyers [ca. 1580] 60

18 William Saunders, autograph letter to Richard Bagot [1585] 62

19 Dinner for the officers of the Exchequer, 1587 64

20 Anne Broughton, letter to her father, Richard Bagot [1587] 66

21 Miles Corbett, autograph letter to John Owles [ca. 1590] 68

22 Sir Nicholas Bacon, address to the serjeants-at-law delivered in 1559 [ca. 1590] 70

23 Robert Devereux, earl of Essex, letter to Sir Edward Littleton and others, 1593 72

24 Richard Broughton, autograph letter to Walter Bagot, 1597 74

25 William Cecil, Lord Burghley, letter to Matthew Hutton, Archbishop of York, 1597 76

26A Examination of Hugh Ford, 1598 78

26B The use of the law [ca. 1600] 78

27 Sir Charles Cavendish, letter to his mother, Elizabeth Talbot, Countess of Shrewsbury [ca. 1600] 80

28 Privy Council, letter to Nathaniel Bacon, 1600 82

29 Sir Robert Cecil, autograph letter to Sir John Peyton [1603?] 84

30 Henry Cavendish, autograph letter to his mother, the Countess Dowager of Shrewsbury, 1605 86

31 Nathaniel Bacon, examination of Stephen Nicholls [1607] 88

32 Privy Council, letter to Sir Arthur Chichester, 1607 90

33 An inventory of the furnishings of Jane Lady Berkeley's London house [1614] 92

34 Lettice Kynnersley, autograph letter to her brother, Walter Bagot [ca. 1615] 94

35 Sir Francis Drake, letter to John Foxe [copied ca. 1615] 96

36 William Wilson, autograph letter to Edward Alleyn [ca. 1617] 98

37 William Herbert, earl of Pembroke, letter to Sir Lionel Tollemache, Bart., 1619 100

38 William Bagot, autograph letter to Walter Bagot, his father, 1622 102

39 William Shakespeare, *Henry IV, Part 1*, II.iv.328–349 [copied ca. 1622] 104

40 The tollbook of Market Bosworth Fair, 1623 106

CONTENTS

41   Philip Holland (probable writer), the coronation of King James
       [ca. 1625]   108

42   A page from a poetical commonplace book [ca. 1630]   110

43   Ben Jonson, satirical verses on Inigo Jones [ca. 1630]   112

44   Richard Napier, autograph letter to an unknown lady [1632]   114

45   Sir Edward Hyde, autograph letter to Sir Marmaduke Langdale [1657] 116

46   W[illiam] L[ane], Petition [1647]   118

47A   de Beau Chesne and J. Baildon, *A New Booke Containing all Sorts of
       Hands* [1611]   120

47B   Martin Billingsley, *The Pens Excellencie* [1618]   120

48   Court roll of the manor court of Hurstmonceux, 1530   122

49   Philip Hoby, bond or note of hand, 1541   124

50   Nicholas Kynnersley, autograph letter to Elizabeth, Countess of Shrews-
       bury, 1588   126

Books Recommended for Reading and Reference   129

ELIZABETHAN
HANDWRITING
1500–1650

A MANUAL

INTRODUCTION

1. The Survival of Manuscripts

Until quite recently all literature, most records, and most communications other than those spoken were written by hand. Since the fifteenth century, literary compositions judged to be of wide interest have, in the main, been put speedily into print, chiefly for the sake of dissemination. And for the same reason certain classes of official records, such as proclamations and statutes, have likewise been printed more or less promptly. Still this is true of no more than a small percentage of official records. Archive and manuscript repositories great and small house millions of written documents as yet unprinted, many unexplored. Historians have not neglected these mines, but neither have they exhausted them, and what riches remain no one knows. Furthermore since editors have not always proved infallible, the manuscript of a printed work retains a practical value for the historian. Wherever exact knowledge of the record is important the original writing will always possess the ultimate authority.

For students of English literature the same importance attaches to an author's original manuscript. But of such literary manuscripts the incidence of survival is much lower than for many classes of historical documents. Why this is so we shall consider presently. The fact is that authors' autograph manuscripts of, say, the sixteenth century have with few exceptions vanished. Of Shakespeare's plays, for example, no manuscript in his autograph is known, and much the same is true of the productions of the other playwrights who worked in the great period of drama from 1580 to 1642. No manuscript of any play has survived in the autograph of Kyd, Greene, Jonson, Chapman, Dekker, Heywood, Marston, Webster, Beaumont, Fletcher, or Ford—to name only the better known dramatists. The facts can be summarized in this way: no play by a professional playwright which was successful on the stage and which was printed before 1642 is known to have come down to our time or near it.*

* There is a manuscript of *The Masque of Queens* in Ben Jonson's autograph, but that is not a play. There are a number of contemporary manuscripts of academic plays (written for production at Oxford or Cambridge), but these were not professional plays and most were not

To understand why some classes of manuscripts have survived in abundance while others have mainly vanished we must inquire into the conditions that have governed preservation or destruction. We may start with a truism: care will be taken to preserve those things recognized as possessing value —and only those things. Recognized value is not always the determining factor, though it is the most important one. Things wanted may be lost through carelessness, accident, or uncontrollable decay. Things not wanted may yet survive if they are not in the way, if they do not speedily decay, *and* if no secondary values lead to their removal or destruction. Huge dumps of worn-out automobiles would not mar the landscape on the outskirts of every big city if the secondary value of scrap iron were high enough to pay for their removal. In discussing the survival of manuscripts, then, we need to assess not only the value attached to the several classes of manuscripts at various times but also such forces as favored their destruction.

Some classes of manuscript records possess an obvious continuing value. A will must be kept safe not only till the testator dies and it is probated but for the indeterminate period during which its provisions may conceivably exert an influence in the disposition of real property—possibly for many generations. Statutes, proclamations, sentences pronounced by courts of law, acts of the Privy Council, treasury and exchequer records —all these and more were recognized at the time of their creation in the Tudor and Stuart age as possessing values extending indefinitely into the future. Failure on the part of government agencies to provide for the preservation of such records could only have led to chaos. A. Agard's *Repertorie of Records* (1631) lists many classes of archives stored in the Tower of London and in the treasury at Westminster—archives going back in long series to the reign of King John (d. 1216). Thomas Powell in his *Direction for Search of Records* (1622) is interested solely in the practical uses of these records for lawyers concerned with disputed titles to land. Because of complex medieval tenures, largely remaining in effect in the seventeenth century, such search was commonly pushed back for centuries.

The practice of keeping records was not confined to the great offices and courts at Westminster but was widespread among men involved in govern-

---

soon printed. A professional play by Philip Massinger, *Believe as You List*, of which the autograph manuscript is preserved in the British Museum, was not successful on the stage and was first printed in 1849. Marlowe's name could appear in the list of playwrights above, but there exists a fragment from a single leaf from the manuscript of his *Massacre at Paris* which may be in his autograph, though this is impossible to prove because the only other specimen of his hand is an early signature. We cannot leave Shakespeare without mentioning a small part of a play which again may be in his autograph: 148 lines in a manuscript play called *Sir Thomas More*, a collaborative effort by several men, of whom Shakespeare seems to have been one. That he was the author of the lines is supported by a good deal of evidence, none of it quite conclusive. That they were written, as we have them, by his own hand is highly probable *if* he was their author. Here, as with Marlowe's *Massacre at Paris*, we have no other writing with which to compare these 148 lines except six unquestionable signatures and two other words, "by me". Signatures, even six of them, are not reliable in comparisons of this sort because they tend to be stylized and formal, bearing little observable relationship to a man's ordinary working hand.

ment at all levels. The justice of the peace in a remote shire was intimately involved in government. He was likely to be a substantial landed gentleman, to be, once or twice, sheriff of his county, also a commissioner for the suppression of recusants or for the breed of horse or for the supply of the royal household. He might be a deputy lieutenant of his county or a vice admiral of a coastal area or the steward of crown estates lying near his seat. In any of these capacities he would be accustomed to receiving letters from the Exchequer, the lord treasurer, or the Privy Council, from the bishop of the diocese or the lord lieutenant or the lord admiral. These letters often required him to take some action—to mediate between two disputants, to apprehend a malefactor, to make a report; they gave him authority to act, and they had to be preserved. In addition he had his own private interests involving records that had to be kept—leases running for a term of years or for a number of lives, marriage settlements, evidences of indebtedness. The safekeeping of these documents was obviously important, and it was possible because their owners lived in big houses where storage presented no problems. These men, having perforce developed the habit of filing important documents, tended to keep even unimportant ones. Also their descendants commonly occupied the same house for many generations, and when an heir succeeded to the ownership of the house and the estate and the attendant responsibilities, it was easier for him to leave undisturbed the inherited bundles of old papers than to sort them out. In short, records were assumed to have some value, they were not in the way, and they would not easily decay.

As examples of family continuity and the preservation of papers we might mention the Cecil family. The first Cecil to attain national prominence was William, Lord Burghley. As lord treasurer for twenty-six years, master of the Court of Wards and Liveries for thirty-seven, and chief minister to Queen Elizabeth, he amassed big estates, built big houses, and accumulated an immense quantity of papers, both official and private. Today these are the property of his descendant, the Marquess of Salisbury, who lives in a house built by the first Lord Burghley's son. On a lower level of importance was Sir William Petre, secretary of state to Henry VIII, Edward VI, and Queen Mary. About 1540 he built a house at Ingatestone, in Essex, and here his descendant, Lord Petre, lives to this day. Still preserved in the house are masses of family muniments and other records, some written before the Norman Conquest. Many other examples could be cited, though the past half century has seen the dissolution of countless great houses and the wanton destruction of tons of records.

It is not to be imagined that the Cecils and the Petres preserved the family papers because they recognized historical value in them. Such recognition may have occurred occasionally, but it was mainly with practical values that these men were concerned. Recognition of historical value in such artifacts is rarely to be found before about the second half of the eighteenth century;

too often the realization that old family archives possessed no practical value resulted in their destruction.

If we take William Shakespeare as a representative of the middle class about whom we happen to know a good deal, we shall find a rather different picture. He sprang from simple yeoman stock. His father came, about 1550, to Stratford-on-Avon, where he became a householder and prospered moderately as a tradesman. William's own prosperity, as playwright, actor, and theatrical businessman, was substantial and came to him early in his life. By 1597, when he was thirty-two and his greatest successes lay ahead of him, he was able to buy New Place, the biggest and most imposing house in Stratford. In this house he spent his last years and died in 1616, and the property passed to his heirs, the last of whom—his last surviving descendant—died in 1670. New Place then passed into alien hands, and about 1702 it was rebuilt and in 1759 was pulled down. Members of the Shakespeare family had lived in Stratford for a hundred and twenty years and in one house for seventy-three. This was obviously neither the kind of house nor the kind of family favorable to the preservation of manuscripts.

The manuscripts of Shakespeare's plays—or anybody else's—were of value only so long as they had a recognized practical value—until, that is, they had been made available in print. Plays in general ranked not as literature but as ephemeral entertainment. Shakespeare himself seems never to have taken steps to obtain for any of his plays the immortality of print. Only about half of them (not including *Macbeth, Othello, Julius Caesar,* or *As You Like It*) were printed in his lifetime. Though many of his plays enjoyed a durable popular success, there is clear evidence that he was not generally regarded as towering over other playwrights of his day. The evidence is to be found mainly in the extant comments made by some fifty of his contemporaries. People were interested in plays and to some extent in actors, but not, so far as the evidence shows, in playwrights. In any case, men did not then pursue hobbies; they did not much collect articles that were not of evident practical value. If they collected signatures and autograph manuscripts they were only those of great men like kings and noblemen. For the author's original manuscript of *Hamlet,* once it had been made available in print, there would have been no market. The heyday of Shakespeare idolatry dawned more than a century after his death.

If the autograph manuscript of *Hamlet* possessed no value as a relic, it did possess value as paper. We must realize that in those days newspapers were unknown, also paper napkins, paper towels, toilet paper, kitchen paper, and so on. What is even more important, wrapping paper, though it existed, was used only for a few special purposes and so was seldom seen by most people. All the paper in England was made by hand, was imported (mainly from France), and was by our standards very expensive. What new paper there was, therefore, could be used in the main only for printing or writing. Paper was available for the packaging of small quantities of pepper, spices, or tobacco, for wrapping fish, starting fires, or a hundred other lowly commercial or domestic uses. But this was used paper, printed or written on, and even it was hard to come by. In a play by Beaumont and Fletcher, *A King and No King*, Bessus, boasting of the number of challenges he received, says that he makes a profit by selling the paper they are written on to the grocers. Bookbinders too used wastepaper—strips to strengthen their hinges, whole sheets laminated to make cardboard or binders' board, half sheets for linings or flyleaves. When these are extant in old books today they consist, with few exceptions, of printed paper or manuscript matter. In London printers and bookbinders were closely associated, for they belonged to the same trade company (or guild), and it is reasonable to assume that a printer would regularly sell his wastepaper to the binder down the street. This waste would consist of sheets spoiled in the printing and also of manuscripts that had, through printing, lost their value as written matter. To the bookbinder the fact that the paper he used bore print or writing was of no concern, and buyers of books must have been equally indifferent to it. The same attitude was evidently held by the housewife or cook, one of the prime consumers of wastepaper. According to a well-authenticated story, John Warburton, a herald and antiquary, about the middle of the eighteenth century deposited in his kitchen a pile of old manuscripts that he wanted, and when he looked for them a year or so later and found only a few remaining, his cook explained that she had used the others to line baking dishes.

Altogether there is abundant evidence to show that used paper was a marketable commodity much in demand for a great variety of uses. This fact by itself sufficiently accounts for the disappearance of certain classes of manuscript matter to which we would attach great importance but in which men three centuries ago recognized no value either as literature or as relics.

2. The Handwriting of the Tudor and Stuart Age

One of the immutable laws of human life is constant change. In speech, in artistic taste, in ethical standards, in manners, each generation differs from the one before it. Handwriting, too, is subject to this principle. The pace of the changes that affect it is inconstant, but it is always slow as compared with that of the changes in, for example, styles of clothing. No two persons write in the same way, and an individual's hand ordinarily changes little between his early maturity and old age.

Fads and fashions arise in handwriting as in clothing, but in handwriting these exert little or no pressure to conform, and therefore they are little felt in a decade or two. A rising new fashion is observable today, a fashion, sometimes called the "new Italian hand," that began in England some two or three decades ago and was diligently fostered by a band of enthusiasts. Its adherents are now numbered in the thousands on both sides of the Atlantic, and in England, where special fountain pens are manufactured to suit the hand, it is taught in many schools. The new hand represents a return to renaissance models. It had its origin in the realization that many of even the most highly literate classes of men, especially in England, had almost lost sight of the function of handwriting and were producing a slovenly and bad-mannered scrawl too often almost wholly illegible.

General changes in handwriting are so slow as to be almost imperceptible except in long retrospect, and even then they are difficult to analyze. Still, in any fifty-year period a general change in English handwriting can be observed—a change sufficient to allow an experienced paleographer to determine with reasonable certainty whether a given specimen was produced close to 1740 or to 1790, 1775 or 1825.

Changes in handwriting vary not only in pace; they vary also in kind. The hand written by English-speaking people since 1700 has belonged to the same class or kind—the same *hand* in the broadest sense, a hand of Italian ancestry. In two hundred and fifty years, while vast revolutions have altered most aspects of human life radically, the changes in the handwriting in this country and in England have been far less drastic than the changes that took place between 1600 and 1700.

The workaday hand of Englishmen in the sixteenth century and to some extent in the first half of the seventeenth is called the *secretary* hand. Martin Billingsley, a professional penman, wrote in *The Pens Excellencie* [1618], that

> the *Secretary* . . . is so tearmed (as I conceiue) partly because it is the Secretaries common hand; and partly also, because it is the onely vsuall hand of England, for dispatching of all manner of bu[si]nesses for the most part, whatsoeuer.

It was used for business both governmental and private, for many kinds of records, for correspondence, for literary composition. Other styles of writing were in use side by side with the secretary for some purposes, but before about 1650 these were exceptional, and the secretary hand was, as Billingsley says, the usual hand. It is with the secretary hand, therefore, that we must be mainly concerned. It was well established by 1525. By 1650 it was well on its way toward extinction, and by 1700 it had vanished—not without trace, but vanished as a distinct hand.

In Elizabethan and Jacobean times men took their handwriting, even the workaday secretary hand, more seriously than is common today. They were taught it in school, and as adults many of them carried on the effort to attain regularity and distinction in their secretary hands. This can be inferred from the written matter surviving, of which the specimens provided in this book may be taken as a fairly representative cross section. Though examples of slovenliness and illegibility will be found, these qualities are proportionately less common than in the handwritten English of our own time. By and large the handwriting of the period we are to deal with is easier to read (once a reasonable familiarity with the hands has been acquired) than that that most of us write or read now. Something of the old attitudes toward handwriting is illustrated in the letter reproduced in Plate 38 below. In the letter by a student at Oxford to his father, it is clear that the father has just complained of the boy's handwriting. The specific complaint was, apparently, that his writing showed "a barren invention," which must mean that it lacked elegance and individuality. The charge is at least in part understandable, because the father, Walter Bagot, much of whose writing has survived, wrote a hand rather less easily legible than his son's but more regular, more highly individual, and more graceful. And there is good reason for thinking that he never relaxed his effort to maintain and even improve these qualities. The evidence lies in the doodling which he did on the backs and in the margins of many of the letters that he received and kept. These doodlings consisted mainly of epigrammatic sentences, proverbial phrases, and sententious quotations from the ancient classics. He always wrote them slowly and carefully, making the lines of writing straight, the slope regular, the spacing even. It is impossible not to conclude that it was the enjoyment of beautiful writing that moved him to perform these exercises.

Of the other hands that existed side by side with the secretary, the most important, as it was to turn out, was the *italic* (or Italian) hand, which in England gained increasing popularity after 1550. Its acceptance was due to two features. The first was its simplicity and the consequent speed with which it could be written without loss of legibility. The second was its grace and beauty, which from the beginning attracted calligraphers (lovers of beautiful writing, artists in handwriting) as it has attracted them ever since. It is these qualities, no doubt, that have imparted to the italic hand the durability we have already mentioned.

In the sixteenth century, and later, writers of the secretary hand often used the italic hand to set off certain elements, such as book titles, or to indicate emphasis. Printers also used italic type for these purposes in the late sixteenth century, and they still do. Some Elizabethan writers learned to write both the secretary and the italic hands. The writer of Plate 16 did; so did Francis Bacon. Sir John Harington wrote beautifully in each, appar-

9

ently preferring the secretary for his letter writing, italic for poetry. One further utility of this hand is explained by Martin Billingsley in *The Pens Excellencie*:

> it is conceiued to be the easiest hand that is written with Pen, and to be taught in the shortest time: Therefore it is vsually taught to women, for as much as they (hauing not the patience to take any great paines, besides phantasticall and humorsome) must be taught that which they may instantly learne?

Whether right or wrong about the reasons, Billingsley was right in saying that women usually learned to write the italic hand (which he called Roman) rather than the secretary; of the autograph letters written by women that survive from the sixteenth century and the first decades of the seventeenth, most are in the italic.

Yet a third class of hands was in use in England for certain purposes during the whole of the age of the secretary hand (and much earlier too). These, known as *court* hands, grew out of a need for relatively fast hands for business, especially the business of the courts and government offices at Westminster. They were usually cursive hands, not without pretentions to elegance. In the course of time certain law courts and government offices developed each its own peculiar variety of court hand, which its clerks were required to learn and to use. There were the Chancery hand, the Common Pleas hand, the Exchequer hand, the Pipe Office hand, and others (examples are shown in Plate 47). Gradually these became frozen or set in form and so have been called *set* hands to distinguish them from free hands—rougher hands used by less well-trained, less specialized scribes.

Developing side by side with these hands and closely related to them were the legal hands, widely used for the transaction of legal business, both private and public. Men connected in one way or another with the law often employed their legal hands for nonlegal writing such as letters (shown in Plate 50). Specimens of other legal hands are provided in Plates 48 and 49.

3. Historical Developments

The ancestry of the secretary hand has not been properly investigated, a fact no doubt connected with the rivalry and ultimate victory of the italic hand. The secretary was in its own day looked upon as a plain working hand with no claim to elegance, and by the close of the seventeenth century, when it was dying, it was beginning to be thought of as belonging to the barbarous gothic age. The name *Roman* applied to some varieties of the italic suggested a respectable ancestry. Italic was brought to England about 1525, was at once recognized for its beauty and easy legibility, and has challenged the best efforts of calligraphers ever since. The italic hand was a foreign importation, the secretary homegrown. If the origins of this native hand have not been fully worked out, some facts about it seem fairly obvious.

The late medieval hands of Western Europe fall mainly into two classes —*book* (or text) hands and court hands. The book hands were used as the name implies, and the fact that they were slow to write did not matter so long as the monastic scriptoria could supply an extremely small demand for books. They must also have been slow to read and hard on men's eyes. These hands are sometimes called *gothic* hands.

Plate 1A provides a small sample of a book hand of about 1400. It is noncursive (the letters not linked), heavy, and angular. Most letters are formed with one penlift, some with two. The ascenders of *b, d, f, h, k, l, t,* and (sometimes) *s,* and the descenders in *g, h, p, q, y, þ, ʒ,* and (sometimes) *r,* are restrained. This feature tends to reduce differences between letters, a difficulty existing also in *m, n, u,* and *i,* especially when these occur in combination together.

The book hand was one of the ancestors of the secretary hand. Another may be recognized in the court hands and the closely related legal hands, which are illustrated in Plates 47–50. But these two hands are not the immediate progenitors of the secretary. A union between them had, at least as early as 1400, produced a hand called the *bastard* hand, a mixture of the court hands and the more formal book hands. In Plate 1B it will be seen to be in some degree cursive, to be written with a fine pen and few penlifts, and to be freer and faster than the book hand. All three of these, book, court, and bastard, flourished, with local variations, throughout Western Europe. The bastard hand is the immediate forebear of the secretary hand.

Because the medieval book hand and the bastard hand lie outside of the main subject matter of this book we have only one specimen of each. The same is true of the court hands proper, illustrated only in Plate 47. Therefore the materials reproduced are inadequate for a satisfactory demonstration of the pedigree we have outlined, and in any case this is not the place for it. Anyone who cares to spend an hour or two at comparing the letters *e, b, d, h, l,* and *r* in Plates 1, 4, 5, 6, 47, 48, and 49 can see something of the relationships described above. It is well to remember that in spite of our use of such terms as *ancestor, progenitor, union, pedigree,* and *bastard,* the analogy between biological genetics and the genetics of manuscript hands is no more than superficial. A style of handwriting is not born; it emerges. And it can acquire characteristics from any hand with which it comes in contact. Thus the secretary hand could have picked up certain letter forms directly from the book hand and the court hand (its grandparents, genetically speaking) as well as through its immediate progenitor, for all of them existed in England at the same time.

The origin of the italic hand is simpler than that of the secretary, also less spontaneous. In the late fourteenth century a number of humanistic scholars, finding increasing difficulty in obtaining good texts of the ancient classics, undertook a quest for a hand faster than the gothic book hands in which such texts were being written. A hand called the *Carolingian minuscule,* developed about the time of Charlemagne, ultimately served as their model for a new hand that so admirably satisfied their requirements as to win acceptance beyond the circle of humanists interested in the propagation of the classics. The hand they developed is known as the *humanistic* script. It tended, like its model, to be vertical but was, unlike its model, cursive, and its letters were in general taller and narrower than those of the Carolingian minuscule and thus more economical of paper or parchment. Both of these hands were written with many penlifts. When written rapidly and without penlifts, as Fairbank and Dickins (see Reading List) were the first to observe, the humanistic script tended to develop a slant, and (because of the characteristics of the edged-quill pen) its rounded arches in *h, m,* and *n* are prone to become pointed, the upstroke being a diagonal connecting link. Thus the humanistic script became italic, which is characterized by absence of penlifts, by the resulting shapes of certain letters, and, commonly but not always, by slant. The relationship of the two hands is not unlike that of roman and italic printing types.

B. L. Ullman with persuasive plausibility dates the first appearance of an italic hand (in Italy) 1423. Its arrival in England appears to have occurred about a century later, and it was thereafter much favored by scholars at Cambridge. Among these Roger Ascham, who was chosen to instruct the Princess Elizabeth in penmanship, was an outstanding practitioner of the hand. These men of course wrote Latin mainly, and during the second and third quarters of the sixteenth century the italic hand was used rather by men of learning and for the writing of Latin than as the common hand of business and correspondence. After that its use became more general; the preference of women (or their teachers) for the italic hand appears to have been established before 1600. By 1577 (Plate 16) we find Richard Broughton writing an italic hand as well as a secretary. By 1590 a substantial number of noblemen were writing it—the earl of Essex (Plate 23) and Lord Burghley (Plate 25) for example.

The italic hand overtook the secretary in popularity before 1650 and ultimately brought about its demise. How this was accomplished is illustrated in Plate 43 and again, in a somewhat more advanced stage, in the earlier Plate 27. In both of these examples some letters are in the italic form, while others retain the pure secretary forms. Other transitional hands showing varying degrees of the tendency to mix italic and secretary are shown in other plates. By 1650 relatively few men, and those mainly of advanced years, were writing pure secretary, and many had abandoned it altogether. It would probably be correct to say, though, that most men were writing a mixed or transitional hand rather than a pure italic.

Little need be said about the history of the court hands and the legal hands because these were outside of the main currents of English hand-writing in the sixteenth and seventeenth centuries. Employment of the court hands in England for the business of several courts was well established by the thirteenth century, and they were still in use beyond the end of the seventeenth.

4. The Mechanics of Writing

SOME LETTERS OF THE SECRETARY HAND

Students of the secretary hand have usually had to content themselves with alphabets showing various forms of each letter. These alphabets are not without value as a starting point, and we accordingly reproduce in Plate 2 one taken from an early guide to handwriting. But such sample alphabets will not by themselves carry the student very far, and the following notes on certain of the letters are designed to help him over some difficulties that may confront him as soon as he starts reading.

C   Though capital *C* will be found in several quite different shapes, one of these may reasonably be called the standard secretary *C*; it can be seen in Plate 19 in the word *Capons* (line 11) and *Codd* (line 15). A good many writers, however, employ this same *C* simply as an initial *c*, apparently having no thought of its being then a capital letter. How the custom arose it is impossible to say. It is not connected with the quite usual use of capitals for important nouns (which continued well into the eighteenth century) or with the merely capricious use of them which we shall often meet. For the *C* may be found as an initial in such insignificant verbs as *can* and *come*, also in adjectives, adverbs, and prepositions, used by writers who show no lack of restraint in the use of capitals in general. In short, this *C* had a dual purpose, sometimes being a normal capital, sometimes a mere initial. In transcribing such initial *C*s it is best to reduce them to lower case (minuscules) if it is ascertainable that they do not conform to the writer's ordinary use of capital letters.

D   Certain forms of capital *D* are used as mere initials in precisely the same way as *C* was, but by fewer writers. Likewise it is best in transcribing to reduce the *D* in these circumstances to lower case. Examples of the usage occur in Plate 12 in *declaringe, due,* and *do* (lines 2, 7, and 18, respectively).

F   Almost all writers agree in using a double minuscule, *ff,* as the capital letter (in Plate 19 compare *Fruicte,* line 19, with *affaires,* line 4).

f   See the notes on *s* below.

i, j   Under the influence of Latin, these two letters (as we consider them to be) were always, at least down to the seventeenth century, regarded as two forms of the same letter. As a consonant (*jump*) the letter was pronounced as we pronounce *j,* but in the sixteenth century most writers and most printers always used *i* instead of *j,* either vowel or consonant, both initially and medially. Of the capital letter only one written form existed, and few printers' fonts seem even to have contained a *J.* In the use of the minuscule, or lower case, there was one situation in which *j* was almost always used, both by writers and by printers, namely in lower-case roman numerals that ended with one or more *is,* for which the final numeral was *j:* thus *xxiij.* Examples may be seen in Plates 6, 15, and 19. In transcribing *J* either *I* or *J* may be used, but not both; *I* is generally preferred.

n   In the secretary hand, as in most medieval hands, most writers usually make no distinction between *n* and *u,* and this sometimes creates difficulties for the transcriber. In Plate 1A the words *manion haunte* (line 2) illustrate the lack of distinction, though the context prevents obscurity. But in Plate 8, line 26, one cannot know with certainty whether the writer intended *personnes* or *persounes.* More serious difficulty may be experienced when we come on *ns* and *us* in conjunction with *ms* and *is,* especially when the *is* are not dotted, as in medieval hands is regularly the case and in sixteenth-century hands frequently. For example, the Latin words *nummum* and *minimum* might well be identical, each consisting of a series of fifteen evenly spaced minims, or single downstrokes.

r   In Plate 1A, two quite different forms of *r* can readily be distinguished. In earlier medieval writing (and in black-letter print down to the eighteenth century) the *r* that occurs in *pride* (line 4) was regularly employed to follow the letters *w, h, y, p, b, o,* and *d* (to use a pronounceable mnemonic order), while other letters were followed by the other *r.* This rule is observed in Plate 1A. In Plate 1B two still different *r*s will be found, one in *Nor* (line 4), the other in *grett* (line 6), and in its terminal form in *fygur* (line

2) and *sur* (line 4). This last *r* is characteristic of court hands and legal hands (illustrated in Plates 47–50) and will not be found in pure secretary hands. The three others reappear in modified forms in secretary. No other letter in secretary hands has so many distinct forms.

s   Every writer of the secretary hand systematically employs two radically different types of *s*—one used initially and medially, the other terminally. This fact can be seen in any of the plates showing secretary hands, but Plate 7 conveniently illustrates several points in connection with this letter. The usual tall initial *s* of the last word in line 1 is preceded by a terminal *s* of the usual form. (What might be taken as a different kind of terminal *s* in the last word of line 9 is in fact not an *s* but a contraction for *es,* which will be discussed later.) In *seased* (line 2) it is possible to see that the *ss* are formed by a thick downstroke to which a curved head is added. This use of two penstrokes is virtually universal in the secretary form of the tall *s*. Even when, as in *shalbe* (line 1), the joining of the head to the shaft cannot be seen, it can safely be assumed. Some writers, instead of actually lifting the pen to add the head, reversed the pen direction at the bottom of the shaft stroke. That Sir William Cavendish did (Plate 7) can be seen in *said* (line 10), *said* (line 12), *Desyrynge* (line 19), and elsewhere. The writer of Plate 6 does it in both ways. In Plate 7 we can see how variously the linking of the tall *s* with a following letter is accomplished. This writer does not link *s* with *a,* usually does with *e,* always does with the ascending letters *h, l,* and *t.* Confusion of the tall *s* with *f* is possible, because by most writers the two letters are formed in precisely the same way—except for one important detail. The head of the *s* may curve down and leftward toward the shaft, but it cannot touch or cross the shaft, since if it does it becomes no longer an *s* but an *f*. Occasionally a writer through inadvertance makes an *f* when he intend *s,* and vice versa, but this is rare.

u, v   Like *i* and *j,* these were regarded, in the Roman alphabet and in English practice till the seventeenth century, not as two letters but as two forms of one letter. Unlike *i* and *j,* they were virtually interchangeable either as consonant or as vowel. Thus we may find the same word written (or printed) *every* and *euery* (though they were pronounced in only one way), also *up* and *vp*. This must not be thought of as a matter of spelling, much less of misspelling; it was simply two ways of writing the same letter —a letter which happened to function as either vowel or consonant, with different pronunciations (just as *y* functions today). There was no rule: either form could be used in any position. But printing-house compositors, who dealt with letters and spellings every day and all day, tended to form habits and to be aware of conventions as they arose. One of these conventions, incipient in the last decades of the sixteenth century, said that *v* was to be preferred initially, *u* medially. Thus *vp* becomes commoner than *up,* *very* commoner than *uery, euery* commoner than *every*. But printers were not unanimous in their observance of such conventions, and in general writers markedly lagged behind printers. Accordingly we find writers who usually use one form or the other pretty consistently, without regard to position, and others who use now one form, now the other, without much rhyme or reason. For the indistinguishability of *u* and *n*, see *n* above.

SPELLING

English schoolboys of the sixteenth century studied Latin, not English. And because Latin had been studied continuously since ancient times and was the language of learning, its syntax, grammar, and spelling were established and relatively immutable. Therefore schoolboys had to learn Latin spelling, which was easy because of the phonetic regularity of the language.

English, on the other hand, was a spoken rather than a written language and, until the fourteenth century at least, had not even been the language spoken by the courtier and the professional man, who used instead Anglo-Norman, a variety of French. For these reasons and because English is highly irregular and nonphonetic in spelling, there was no such thing as "correct" orthography in the early sixteenth century, when education and literacy were only just beginning to touch large numbers of people. Any spelling that would clearly indicate a particular spoken word was good enough. For most people a word was a sound or a series of sounds, not a prescribed series of letters. The words *right* and *wrong* were hardly applicable to spelling. That the writer of the document shown in Plate 14 wrote *bargayned* in line 8 and *bargaine* in line 9 would not have attracted the least notice, and it is no more remarkable that Shakespeare spelled his name in several different ways.

From the early sixteenth century, as more and more persons learned to read and write, their feelings about words began to change. They began noticing the spellings they saw in print and were influenced by them, and thus standardization of English spelling began. It affected first the common short words that provide little scope for variation. Before about 1625 the pace was slow, the progress slight; the latter half of the seventeenth century brought the most rapid progress toward a standard spelling, which has not yet been fully achieved. In the whole movement printing-house compositors played a leading role, because spelling was their job and they tended to form habits, and also because of the influence of the printed word. In all periods the spellings found in printed English can be seen to be less free, less erratic than in written. Similarly, educated men, especially men who wrote much, tended to spell less erratically than men of small education; and women, who by and large had little opportunity for education, were markedly more erratic than their husbands and brothers.

It would be virtually impossible to deal systematically with the spelling of that time, and this is not the place for the attempt. We can, however, point out some of the more conspicuous ways in which sixteenth-century spelling differs from our own.

Perhaps the first thing to strike one's notice will be the almost random addition of terminal *es*. In the first six lines of the letter in Plate 18 we can find the following examples: *losse, frende, worlde, whome, nowe, fatherlesse, motherlesse*. We shall also run into the omission of final *es* to which we are accustomed: *com, gon, mak, mad,* and the like.

The doubling of certain consonants is common: *allways, comme, triffling, fasshion, principall;* also the undoubling, as in *wel, wil, unles, goodnes, maner* (for *manner*). Similarly we shall find the vowels *e* and *o* both doubled and undoubled: *oone, twoo, shee, wee, goone, shooe, hoorse,* and *thre, kne, gode, fote*.

In English one vowel sound may be spelled in several ways. Thus *leave, believe, receive* all rhyme. In sixteenth-century usage the second syllable of *believe* is commonly spelled in all three of these ways and also *beleeve*. Such vowel interchanges may be found in infinite variety in that century, and we can point out only two or three. The *o/ou* change is very common, as in *wold* for *would, gould* for *gold, cold* for *cold* or *could, could* for *could* or *cold*. The interchanging of *i, y,* and *ie* will be found in almost every line of writing. The substitution of *w* for *u* is almost as common: *yow* occurs about as often as *you*, and we shall frequently find *owt, abowt, howse, prowd,* and *thowsand*.

Consonant interchanges are less common, of course. The interchanging of *c, k,* and *ck* is one of the commonest, as in *public, publike, publick, lik* and *lick* for *like*, and *sik* for *sick*. The *c/t* interchange deserves special mention. For this there is a linguistic reason, and it is common to Romance languages. In learning Latin in this country we are taught to pronounce *ratio* with a plain *t* sound—the "classical" pronunciation. But in some continental European countries and in church-Latin here, this is pronounced with a *ts* sound. In modern Italian we have *razione,* with the same *ts* sound; in French *ration,* with an *s* sound; in Spanish *ración*. In English the suffix *tion* has an *sh* sound, and the same sound is in *gracious* (from Latin *gratia*). So in early modern English we come across both *gracious* and *gratious, special* and *spetial, action* and *accion*. It is this interchangeability of *c* and *t* that accounts for the conventional contraction *con*, usually with a tittle, for *tion* (*cion*). For an explanation of the tittle see page 19.

PUNCTUATION

Like the spelling, the punctuation of the Tudor and Stuart period is different from ours. Attempts have been made to analyze the dramatic punctuation found in the First Folio edition of Shakespeare, but these were largely futile because they were based on the assumption that the punctuation was Shakespeare's own rather than, as it is now held to be, the printers'. Responsibility for punctuation (as for spelling) was forced upon the printing-house compositors by the erratic punctuation employed by most writers. If the 148 lines of *Sir Thomas More* commonly attributed to Shakespeare were actually written in his autograph, it is apparent that he had no grasp of the function of punctuation as we understand it today or as the first printers of his other plays understood it. The 148 lines are almost without punctuation.

Those 148 lines cannot be said to be typical of Elizabethan punctuation in general; they are only one specimen of it. The specimens provided in our plates may be taken as a fair cross section, illustrating the two extremes, from total absence of punctuation in Plate 3 and the almost total absence in Plate 11 to the largely meaningless scattering of full stops and colons by Lettice Kynnersley in Plate 34, also many degrees in between.

Writers between 1500 and 1650 used all of the marks of punctuation in use today, but with observable differences. Semicolons will be met with only rarely, colons far more than today. Question marks were used then as we use them, but also they were used where we use exclamation points. These last were latecomers, being almost unknown before 1650. Quotation marks were seldom used before 1600, and then rather to call attention to a phrase or a sententious expression than to mark direct quotation.

Commonly before 1580, not often after 1600, we find a mark of punctuation that was to pass out of use entirely, namely the virgule, /. By the sixteenth century it was equivalent to a comma, except when it stood at the end of a section, chapter, or whole composition, sometimes two or three together, sometimes bracketed by periods. Hyphens were used much as they are now, except that when placed at the end of a line to indicate a break they are usually double, = (like an equal sign), often slanted, sometimes placed below the base line (examples in Plates 12, 30, 46, and others). Numerals, both roman and arabic, will often be found to be both preceded and followed by periods. A mark that cannot really be classed as punctuation was commonly placed at the end of a line to fill space (examples in Plates 11, 14, 22, 32, 36, and others). This takes many shapes but is usually curved, curled, or looped.

ABBREVIATION AND CONTRACTION

In the Middle Ages, when costly parchment was the only available writing material, there was a strong motive for the packing of the greatest possible number of words into each line. As an aid in this compression there grew up a convention of copious abbreviation (the cutting off of the ends of words) and contraction (the omission of medial letters and elements) —

devices to which Latin lent itself rather better than English did. In Plate 48, line 7, the first five words are "homag ibm psent qd Iohes", standing for "homagium ibidem presentat quod Iohannes". The first word is abbreviated, the others contracted, the third word both abbreviated and contracted. The following are standard contractions of some common words: *dnus* for *dominus, hoi* for *homini, hoibus* for *hominibus, dia* for *dimidia, Michas* for *Michaelmas*. Often these abbreviations and contractions were indicated by a mark of some sort at the end or wherever omission occurred. The commonest mark of abbreviation was an upward and backward stroke attached to the last letter written, and there were also downward strokes.

At the opening of the sixteenth century in England the general use of abbreviation and contraction persisted, like so much else that was medieval, even though the need for them had become less acute as paper became more available. In the writing of English, contraction was now managed mainly in two ways: first, in the use of signs and symbols carried over from medieval Latin, second, in the use of superior (supralineal) letters, usually the terminal letter or letters of a word or syllable.

y^e   This contraction, perhaps the commonest of all after 1500, originated in the fifteenth century with a purely English ancestry. This origin is clearly illustrated in the two parts of Plate 1. In 1A, line 3, is the word þe (*the*), the first letter of which is the Old English thorn, originally representing the voiceless *th* sound as in *thorn*, though by the late fourteenth century it was much used for the voiced *th*, as it is in 1A. In Plate 1B, line 1, the same word is written with a *y* in place of a thorn. From the thorns in 1A it is easy to see how the change to *y* came about, for a number of the thorns look like *y*s, notably the one in line 3. In the course of the fifteenth century, perhaps influenced after 1450 by continental printed matter, the old-fashioned thorn was dropped except in the contractions of the particles *the, they, this, that,* sometimes *them, their,* and *those,* and rarely other words in *th.* These, but particularly *the,* were by 1500 so well established as standard contractions, now written with *y,* that they persisted through the seventeenth century.

&   Among the commonest and most durable of the contractions was the ampersand (a corruption of *and per se and,* i.e., *&* by itself makes *and*). It was made in a number of ways.

e   This very common symbol stands for *es* or *is.* It was used, right up to 1650 and beyond, for plurals of nouns and for possessives where we would use *s* or *'s.*

Tittle   This is a short line, straight, wavy, or looped, made over a letter or letters. The commonest use of it in the sixteenth century and later is to indicate omission of an *m* or *n* at the end of a word or syllable; for this, the tittle is placed over the letter preceding the omitted letter. Thus we shall

19

find $\bar{\imath}$ for *in* (Plate 1A, line 3), *mā* for *man* and *mē* for *men* (Plate 1B, line 3, and Plate 5, line 6), *coṁmytted* for *commytted* (Plate 7, line 25), *cōfort* for *comfort* (Plate 18, line 4). In earlier times the tittle was used to indicate many kinds of contraction; in the sixteenth century it is not often found except for *m* and *n* and in one other use. That is the contraction of *tion* to *con* (see p. 19). In the first lines of letters shown in Plates 5, 7, 11, 12, 18, and others, the word *commendations* is so contracted, as are also *sollicitation* (Plate 23, line 7), *computation* (Plate 16, line 16), and *nation* (Plate 13, line 16). In Plate 14, line 8, and Plate 2B, line 5, are examples of less common uses of the tittle. Writers were not usually careful to make their tittles precise in length, and we can find examples extending over a whole word or more. A common variety consists of an upward-backward curve from a final letter. And the beginning reader needs to be warned that some writers made tittles for no reason at all. When we come upon *evon* with a tittle over the *n* (Plate 11, line 1) we can hardly suppose that the writer intended *evonn* (for *even*); *kinsmann* (Plate 13, line 23) seems equally unlikely; and the tittle over *Raigne* (Plate 14, line 1) has no possible meaning.

er, ir, or, ur   The contraction for these letters appears in so many forms and varieties that it is not practicable to reproduce them here. At least three varieties can be seen in Plate 5, in *After* (line 1), *ther* and *other* (lines 7 and 12), and in *pleasur* and *serve* (lines 3 and 7). Precisely the same character that this man uses for *er* in *After,* he also uses for plain *r* in *torne* (line 7) and *right* (line 1). Strictly speaking we might call this an error, but to be quite fair we should say that one form of *r* found in medieval writing, and occasionally in the sixteenth century, is similar to the *er* symbol, and it is probable that the two had become confused.

ꝑ (or ꝓ, ꝑ)   These symbols, medieval in origin, stand respectively for *per* and *pro;* at least that is the theory. Actually many writers in the sixteenth century made little distinction and used either symbol for either syllable. The *per* symbol is not used for the prefix only but will be found for the second syllable of words like *proper* and *paper.*

9   Finally among contraction symbols this one, for *us,* is common in Latin but rare in English, because the combination does not appear as a suffix. In Plate 1B, line 7, it is used for *ous.* A symbol for *con* (9) is quite similar.

These symbols were carried over from medieval Latin. Sixteenth-century English had its own home-grown variety of contraction. The pattern was one or two initial letters with one or more terminal letters written in the superior position. The following are some of the commoner contractions formed on this pattern:

M[r] *for* Master (*not* mister)
M[ris] *for* Mistris (Mistress)

S^r *for* Sir
K^t *for* Knight
Matie *for* Majestie
A^o D^{ni} *for* Anno Domini
wth *or* w^t *for* with
y^r *or* y^{or} *for* your.

In practice almost any fairly common word could be contracted in this way. Superior letters will often be found written directly over the inferior initial letter (as in Plate 30, line 1). The fondness for superior letters led rather often to their use when no saving or any other object was effected. A curious form of this is an *a* written above the suffix *aunt* or *aunce,* not uncommonly in a form similar to that in *waraunt* in Plate 5, line 14. We also find *ou^r* for *our, afte^r* for *after, iiij^{or}* for *four* (Plate 6, line 25), and *xx^{tie}* for *20.* The raising of *r* and certain other elements to indicate contraction was so common that writers simply fell into the habit of raising some final part of a word that ended in *r, th,* and so on. A comparable meaningless habit consisted of making tittles over words or parts of words where these served no function (well illustrated in Plate 13, where, however, many of the tittles do have a function).

Abbreviation was also used in both printing and writing a good deal more freely than is the custom now. Some of the commoner abbreviations are:

Lo. *for* Lord, Lords, Lord's, Lordship, Lordship's
Ho. *for* Honor, Honors, Honorable, and so on
La. *for* Lady, Ladyship, and so on
Io. *for* Iohn (John)
Tho. *for* Thomas
Ia. *for* Iames (James)
Wa. *for* Walter
Hen. *for* Henry
l. *or* li., s., d. *for* pounds, shillings, pence
viz. *for* videlicet (namely).

Instead of a period after abbreviation, we shall often find a colon.

5. Editorial Principles

An early manuscript can be transcribed in print in various ways. At one extreme lies the completely modernized text, reproducing the content only —all spellings modernized; punctuation, abbreviation, and the use of capitals standardized; contractions expanded. At the other extreme lies the nearest approach to facsimile reproduction that is attainable in type, a kind of printing which requires hand setting in a shop equipped with a great number of special type sorts—symbols, signs, and marks employed by medieval writers and still used in the sixteenth century. Examples of this kind of printing can conveniently be seen in the Malone Society's *Collections II.1* (1913), *II.3* (1931), and *III* (1954).

Inherent in fully modernized text is the disadvantage that the transcriber must also constantly be an editor; he must interpret, and in so doing he may often alter the writer's meaning. A further disadvantage lies in the loss, in such modernized texts, of linguistic detail important to some students. On the other hand, the production of a type facsimile is today so costly that books so printed can seldom pay their own way, and since, at best, the type reproduction of early manuscripts cannot be completely accurate and reliable, those who require detailed reproduction of this sort usually prefer photographic reproductions of originals, which are now usually obtainable without prohibitive cost. For the majority of students a modernized text or a compromise between the two extremes is satisfactory.

The transcripts accompanying the plates in this book have, of course, a special purpose, and this has dictated the editorial policies that we have adopted. While scrupulously adhering to original spelling and punctuation, we have thought it best to expand most abbreviations and contractions, which, left as written, would require constant glossing. This expansion is done silently, without any signal, on the assumption that in each instance it will be immediately apparent. We depart from this practice when dealing with contractions now familiar to everyone, so retaining *Mr* and *&*. We also make exception (mainly in plate 48) in a few cases where the writer has omitted a Latin inflection ending and where there is no way of determining which of two or more possible endings the writer had in mind. Here, following the now accepted practice in transcribing medieval and renaissance Latin, we indicate the omission by a supplied apostrophe. Where we do expand contractions and abbreviations we use the spelling favored by the individual writer if this can be inferred. In expanding an abbreviation we ignore any sign such as a period, a colon, or a flourish.

Acting on a similar principle, we silently lower most superior letters. Thus we print *Mr*, not *M*^{r}. But again we make exceptions where the lowering of a superior letter would cause confusion, as it would if the abbreviations for *pounds, shillings,* and *pence* were lowered in expressions of amounts of money (as in Plates 6 and 19). Meaningless tittles we of course ignore in transcription. Another custom of no practical utility but deeply ingrained in most Elizabethan writers is the crossing of *l* and especially *ll*. Though used by some writers only for special purposes, these can nevertheless be regarded as no more than forms of the letter, and accordingly we always transcribe them as a plain *l* or *ll*.

A problem that has to be faced by the transcriber of any handwriting from the late fifteenth century to the late eighteenth is the treatment of certain initial letters. These are the letters of which the capitals and the minuscules are formed in the same way and differ only in size, the number of them varying with individual writers, since every capital has more than one shape. The problem arises when capital and minuscule vary only a little in size, or do not vary at all. The transcriber of course wants to adhere to the writer's intention, and if the writer leaves this in doubt, the transcriber can only make a more or less arbitrary choice. But he should not be purely arbitrary unless the writer shows himself to be wholly capricious in his use of capital letters. The letters that may give this trouble are *c, g, k, m, n, o, s, u, v, w,* and *y*. After about 1800, when the use of capitals came to be pretty well standardized, the problem will hardly arise.

Another problem in the solution of which a transcriber is sometimes forced to make arbitrary choices has to do with spaces between words. Most writers leave some of the letters in some words unjoined, and some leave most unjoined. If in addition to leaving many letters unjoined a writer tends to leave little or no space between words, then difficulties will arise. In Tudor and Stuart times words that we always separate were often intentionally joined as one word: *shalbe, evenso, noman*. Conversely we find *some what, every body, how so ever*. It is with words like these that problems arise in the work of a writer obviously careless about linkage and spaces. If such a one seems to join impossible words this can only be regarded as accident, not intention, and treated accordingly.

In the transcripts in this book we use square brackets only to enclose interpolated matter—a letter or a word omitted through carelessness and needed to help the sense, also (rarely) an interpolation of a word of our own helpful to the sense. We use broken brackets ⟨ ⟩ to indicate deleted matter. If the deleted matter is legible we enclose it, if not we leave the brackets empty. Careted interlined matter we silently insert in the place indicated; in the absence of a caret we place the matter where it seems to belong—

with a note if this is doubtful. Where deleted matter carries interlined substitute matter above it, we print the latter immediately after the broken brackets.

Of the fifty-four specimens shown in the plates, more than half reproduce whole pieces—letters, deeds, or documents. Of the others, some are brief excerpts from long poems or plays; some contain the opening lines of a letter, a poem, a speech, or a document; some fall only a line or two short of completeness. If the incompleteness of an extracted or truncated item is not self-evident, we mention it in a headnote. In twelve instances less than the whole of the amount of text reproduced is transcribed, and this is indicated by three dots printed beneath the last line of transcript.

The title line of each transcript contains the date or the approximate date of the handwriting. Usually this is also the date of composition, but for eleven it is not (Plates 1A, 8, 17, 22, 26B, 35, 39, 41, 42, 43). A date printed without square brackets is one that actually appears in the text reproduced. Dates between December 31 and March 25 we express in the modern way. The almost invariable practice in England down to about the end of the seventeenth century was to change the year-date not on January 1 but on March 25. Thus the day after 31 December 1601 was 1 January 1601, and the next March 24 was still 1601 and was followed by 25 March 1602. We alter such dates to conform to present-day usage. In Plate 23, where Essex dates his letter 2 March 1592, we print *1593* in the title, and we treat the date of Burghley's letter, Plate 25, in the same way.

6. Methods of Study

We have earlier discussed various shapes of certain letters in the secretary hand (pp. 13–14). Neither there, however, nor in the notes to the transcripts would it be possible to discuss all the shapes that may be found.

One reason for this is the effect of linkage. An *i* followed by a tall *s* and linked to it is likely to assume a form not to be found in other situations; in some hands an *o* takes on a peculiar form when linked to a preceding *t*. Many other examples of this sort of thing could be listed.

Again, Elizabethans were deeply imbued with a love of style and decoration, observable in their poetry and their prose, their music, and their architecture. Their handwriting exhibits this same ornateness, and the secretary hand lent itself well to the expression of it. And when carried to excess, as it often was, in exuberant loops, exaggerated spurs, or great slashing descenders, the result may be a reduction of legibility.

Yet a major factor producing the almost infinite variety in the forms of letters is individuality—the fact that no two persons write in just the same way. And most writers are prone to fall now and then into slovenliness when they are in a hurry—to form letters carelessly or not at all. Many writers of our own time tend to flatten out an *m* or the word *in* till it is little more than a straight line. Others will represent an *e* or *r* or *s* indifferently by a mere hump. Only by experience do we learn to read this kind of writing when it is produced by our contemporaries. And only by experience, by acquiring a familiarity with the commoner, more usual forms of the secretary letters, can we hope to read badly malformed specimens.

Experience with handwriting consists of reading it. But first we must look closely at the letters. An exhaustive examination of all varieties and combinations of letters is not needed at the start, though it is in this direction that the first steps ought to be taken. Here a reading glass or small magnifying glass is a desirable tool. Now we might begin with the vowels. Turning to Plate 22, a clear, carefully written hand, let us look at some specimens of the letter *a*, finding them in the transcript and examining them in the reproduced text. In *vnderstanding*, line 4, the *a* is made in two parts with a penlift: first a c-shaped curve, the penlift, then the final downstroke, which starts with a small horizontal lefthook at the top and bends right at the bottom. Looking below, we shall find the *a* in *that*, line 5, to be made in the same way except that the horizontal lefthook is longer. Coming back to line 4, we find the *a* in *as* made quite differently—in one stroke looping around clockwise from upper right to lower right, like a Greek alpha. The *a* in the contracted *Maiesty*, line 12, though less clear appears to be made in the same way. The *a* in *and*, line 5, is of a third kind, starting with a long spur, or attacking stroke, that begins at the tip of the *d*. The spur is light because the pen was moving on a course parallel to its edge; it terminates in a closed loop; then follows a short stroke, down to the right and heavy because the direction has changed; next a light upstroke, right, and a final heavy downstroke. If we look further it will appear that the spurred *a* is used only initially, though not all initial *a*s are spurred. Perhaps now we should turn to other specimens to see if other writers tend to use spurred *a*s initially only.

This brief examination of a few *a*s will serve to demonstrate the most effective way of developing an eye for the varying shapes of letters— working out pen movements and penlifts, always comparing, trying to see the peculiar habits of each writer. After the vowels it would be well to tackle the high-frequency consonants *r* and *s*, each of which occurs in a number of fairly distinct forms. Then it would be profitable to pay special attention to certain letters that are subject to confusion with other letters: *e* and *d*, *e* and *i*, *e* and *o, n* and *u, s* and *f*. Close attention to letters in pairs, to observe how linkage affects the shapes of letters: *ct, ng, pr, si, st, cc, ff, oo, ss*. A useful exercise is the forming of letters oneself with pencil or pen, compiling an alphabet of the several more distinct forms of each letter.

This kind of close examination of letters should never be dropped, even after one has acquired a facility in reading. But a start at reading should not be long deferred. After no more than an hour of close letterwork, the student would be well advised to begin reading one of the clearer, easier hands shown in Plates 14, 18, 19, and 22. At first, reliance upon transcripts will be almost total and progress slow. Later, as more and more familiarity with the letters is gained through alternate reading and letterwork, increasing independence will come. The learner may then be ready to read on his own some of the specimens not fully transcribed (Plates 7, 16, 18, 27, 34, 35, 40, 42, 44, 46, 48).

We were speaking of hasty and slovenly writing as a factor producing illegibility. Every writer has his hasty moments, and malformed letters, careless omissions, and the like will be met with constantly (see note 16 to Plate 20 and note 10 to Plate 6). The failure to differentiate between certain pairs of letters, like *e* and *o* (note 8 to Plate 8) or *e* and *i* (see the headnote to Plate 36 and the note to line 1) is a special kind of carelessness. We can hardly count as carelessness the confusion of *n* with *u*, because few writers ever made a distinction between them. The mending or altering of letters or larger elements is another source of minor illegibilities (see, for example, the notes to Plate 3, lines 5 and 11; Plate 7, line 14; Plate 14, line 18; Plate 20, line 15). Of the several kinds of damage to paper—tears, trimming, chafing, blots, mildew, worms—all of which at times produce illegibility, most are not illustrated in the plates (but see the note to Plate 39, line 4).

From these examples of illegibility it will be apparent that the transcriber of handwritten text cannot always expect to arrive at an unquestionable reading of a letter or a word. He is forced to resort now and then to conjecture. He can usually arrive, with patience and ingenuity backed by paleographic and linguistic experience, at a convincing conjecture. Many of our notes on uncertain readings will serve to illustrate the various ways of arriving at more or less satisfactory solutions to these problems. Context alone will often, perhaps usually, suggest an evidently correct reading. The desired goal is to reconstruct precisely what the writer wrote, meant to write, or thought he was writing. In striving for this goal an appeal to analogy is frequently the best method—analogy to a writer's habitual spelling habits (notes to Plate 36, line 5; Plate 16, line 10) or to other examples of his way of forming a particular letter (see notes to Plate 18, line 6; Plate 29, lines 1 and 3). Another kind of analogy is illustrated in the note to Plate 12, line 6.

PLATES AND TRANSCRIPTS

1A ROBERT MANNYNG OF BRUNNE
AN EXTRACT FROM HANDLYNG SYNNE [CA. 1400]

This long poem was composed about 1300. The hand is discussed on page 11.

Þer was a kniȝt þat loued nouelrie
as manion haunte now þat folie.
he dede do make him in þe someris tide
a kote perced queinteli with pride.
& god was not þer of paide   5
for in his pride he was betraide.
þis kniȝt ȝede vpon a dai
a boute robbori to gete his prai.
                        • • •

2 *manion*] many one.

1B AN EXTRACT FROM MIND, WILL, AND UNDERSTANDING
A MORALITY PLAY [CA. 1460]

The extract is the opening of a long speech by Will. *The hand is discussed on page 11.*

And I of the soull am the wyll
Off the godhede lyknes & fygur
Wyt goode wyll no man may spyll
Nor wyt owt goode wyll of blys be sur
Wat soule wyll gret mede recur   5
He must grett wyll haue in ⟨dede & or⟩ thought or dede
Wertuusly sett wyt consyens pur
For in wyll stondyt only mannys dede
Wyll for dede oft ys take
Therfor the wyll must weell be dysposyde   10

4 *wyt*] In expanding the contraction we follow the scribe's usual spelling, common in the fifteenth century; cf. also *stondyt* in line 8.
5 *recur*] recure, i.e., obtain.

6 The inclusion of *in* with the deleted words is obviously an error.
7 *Wertuusly*] For the contraction of us, the third syllable, see page 20.

Þer was a kniȝt þ loued nouȝtrie
As maniou þ annte volde þ false.
He dede do make hl i þe someris tide
A cote pred queintell ut pride,
& god was not þer of paide
for i his pride he was betrasde.
þis kniȝt ȝede vpon a dai
a boute roȝȝou to gete his prai.
Homward as his prai he ledde
Uf his euemis he was bestedde.
Uf force þei gune uf him to fiȝte
& slouȝ þere þis iche kniȝte.
þe kniȝtes freudes herde seie
how he was slain be þe weie.
ful seire for hl þa gune þei werche
þe beried þe bodi seire at þe cherche.
His freudis departede his catel
a mẽdui þei wisȝ it was wel.

And i of þo soule dui þo wytt
Off þo godhede kẽudõ & freud
wyt goode wytt no mã mdy spyll
for it out goode wytt of ȝlyȝ þo luȝ
wat soule wytt ȝet mode þou̅
he must ȝ̃dtt wytt ham in dede & honest̃ dede
wortuiȝ sott it toȝ ouo puȝ
ffor m wytt stõdyt euly nidmȝ dede
wytt for dede oft þo takȝ
þerfor þo wytt must woott be dysposede

2A

J. DE BEAU CHESNE AND J. BAILDON
A WOODCUT ENGRAVING FROM A BOOKE
CONTAINING DIVERS SORTES OF HANDS [1571]

The secretarie Alphabete.

A a a a A A A a a a A A b b b B B B B c c C C cc
C d d d d d d D D D e e e E E E f F f
F F G g g g g g G h h h H H h h H I I I
K k k k k l il L L mmm M N M N m m M N   5
O o o oo O O p pp P P P P P q q q que Q Q Q
R R R r r r R r r S S S s s s ss s s st st st st st
T t tt T v w W V u u w v W V w v w w v u
V W x x x X y y Y y y Z z z z & & & & us us us

3 *d*] On the fourth *d* see p. 14.

2B

J. DE BEAU CHESNE AND J. BAILDON
A NEW BOOKE, CONTAINING ALL SORTS OF HANDS [1611]

A small rounde secretary.
Three thinges are to be pitied, and the fourth not to be suffered. A good
manne in the handes of a tyraunt. A wise manne vnder the gouernaunce of a foole. A liberall manne in subiection to a wretche or a
catife. And a foole sett in aucthoritie. This sayth Hermes the ph[ilosoph]or.   5
A a a b b c cc d d e e e f' f g g h h I i ij k k l ll n mm.
n nn o oo p p q q r r r s s st t tt v v w u w x y z & us.

3 *manne*] The tittle over the second *manne* is meaningless and superfluous; see pp. 19–20.

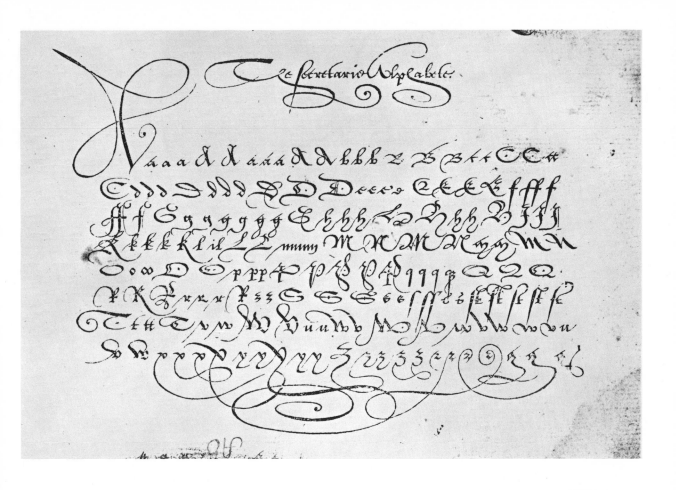

The Secretarie Alphabete.

A small romane secretary.

Three thinges are to be pitied, and the fourth not to be suffered. A good manne in the handes of a tyraunt. A wise manne vnder the gouern-aunce of a foole. A liberall manne in subiection to a wretche or a catife. And a foole sett in authoritie: This sayth Hermes the phor.

3   A DEED CONVEYING LAND 1501

This is a deed conveying an estate in fee-simple written in a legal hand.

Sciant presentes et futuri quod ego henricus Ferman de Nethercote in Comitatu Warwici dedi concessi et hac
presenti Carta mea confirmaui Thome Pereson vnam acram terre iacentem in Campis de Nethercote
predicto Salbrygg et Wolfhamcote in Comitatu predicto quarum quidem acrarum vna dimidia acra iacet apud le Red Cros
que iacet iuxta heywey et alia dimidia acra iacet in le Eammys que iacet iuxta terram domini de Nethercote habendum
et tenendum predictam acram cum suis pertinenciis predicto Thome heredibus et assignatis suis imperpetuum de Capitalibus 5
dominis

feodi illius per seruicia inde debita et de iure consueta Et ego vero predictus henricus et heredes mei predictam acram cum
suis pertinenciis predictis prefato Thome heredibus et assignatis suis contra omnes gentes warantizabimus acquietabimus et
imperpetuum defendemus Et insuper sciatis me prefatum henricum fecisse ordinasse et loco meo posuisse dilectos michi
in Christo Iohannem Quyney et Ricardum Roberdes meos veros et legittimos attornatos coniunctim et diuisim adiutandum
in predictam acram terre cum suis pertinenciis predictis et quascumque alias personas inde expellere et asseisina ac possescione 10
inde totaliter amonere et plenaream ac pacificam possescionem et seisinam inde vice et nomine meo predicto Thome
secundum vim formam tenorem et effectum presentis Carte mee deliberandum Ratum et gratum habentem et habiturum totum
et quicquid

dicti attornati mei nomine meo fecerint seu alter eorum fecerit in premissis In cuius rei testimonium huic presenti
Carte mee sigillum meum apposui Datum tercio die mensis decembris Anno regni regis henrici septimi
post conquestum septodecimo hiis testibus Ricardo Quyney Iohanne Letes Iohanne Curtes et aliis multis 15

5 *acram*] The first part of the word is written over an erasure.   11 *amonere*] The first *e* is written over another letter.

Sciant presentes et futuri quod ego Henricus Forman de Netherecote in com. Warrewic' dedi concessi et hoc
presenti carta mea confirmavi Thome Persson unam acram terre iacentem in campis de Netherecote
predict' Solbrugg' et Wolfhamcote in com. predicto quarum quidem acrarum una dimidia acra iacet apud le Redehos
que vocatur Hegthey et alia dimidia acra iacet in le Sichinges que vocatur iuxta terram dni de Nethercote Habend'
et tenend' predictam acram cum suis pertinentiis predicto Thome heredibus et assignatis suis imperpetuum de capitalibus dominis
feodi illius per servicia inde debita et de iure consueta. Et ego vero predictus Henricus et heredes mei predictam acram cum
suis pertinentiis predictis prefato Thome heredibus et assignatis suis contra omnes gentes warantizabimus et acquietabimus et
imperpetuum defendemus. Et insuper sciatis me prefatum Henricum fecisse ordinasse et loco meo posuisse dilectos michi
in Christo Johannem Curteys et Ricardum Walsshe meos veros et legittimos attornatos coniunctim et divisim ad intrand'
in predictam acram terre cum suis pertinentiis predictis et quascumque alias parcellas inde capiendas et deliberand' ac possessionem
inde totaliter amovendam et plenariam ac pacificam possessionem et seisinam inde vice et nomine meo predicto Thome
secundum vim formam et effectum presentis carte mee deliberand' ratum et gratum habentem et habiturus totum et quicquid
dicti attornati mei nomine meo fecerint seu alter eorum fecerit in premissis. In cuius rei testimonium huic presenti
carte mee sigillum meum apposui. Dat' tercio die mensis Decembris Anno regni regis Henrici septimi
post conquestum septimodecimo hiis testibus Ricardo Curteys Johanne Webbe Johanne Emtys et aliis multis

4

HENRY VIII, WARRANT 1525

This document, written by a scribe but bearing the king's signature, or, more properly, his sign manual at the top, shows at a very early date an almost fully developed secretary hand, with traces of earlier book hands only in some rs and some final ss. Perhaps to cancel the document, the right end was cut off, and later (probably in the nineteenth cen- tury) a spurious restoration was attempted by someone with small paleographic skill and less knowledge of old documents. No such royal castle as Warborough (Wargboroughe? Warhboroughe?) is known. We attempt a more plausible restoration.

Henry Rex

Henry the eight by the grace of god king of England and of Fraunce defensour of [the faith and lord of Ireland]
To the Treasorer and Chambrelains of oure Eschequier greting / Forasmoche as we haue [commanded the feast of Saint]
George Patron of the noble ordre of the Garter to be kept within our Castell of W[indsor on the thirtieth day]
of this present moneth of Iune next comyng / We therfor woll and commaunde [that out of any the]
Treasour and money resting in your handes ye content paye and deliuere vnto o[ur trusty and wellbeloved]   5
seruant Iohn Shirley Coferer of oure houshold the some of oon hundred markes [sterling to pay the costs]
and charges of the said fest / without any prest or other charge to be sette vpon [it by any person whatever and]
these our lettres shalbe youre sufficient warraunt and discharge in that behalf [Witness our hand and]
seel at our Citie of london the xix daye of Iune / The Seventeneth yere of ou[r reign]   10

2 *eight*] The stroke over this word is meaningless, as are others in this document.

6 *deliuere*] On the *d* see Introduction page 14.
9 *discharge*] The *e* is obscured by damage to the document.

James R

James the eight by the grace of god king of England and of ffraunce
& Ireland of the faith defendor and Chamberlaine of our Exchequer greeting fforasmuch as we have geven . . .
George Barron of the noble order of the Garter to be kept them our Castell of Northborowgh
the present moneth of June next comyng We therfore will and commaund that the
Treasurer and money reigning in your handes ye content paye and deliver unto our Trusty
Sirrth John Chynbye Esquire of our houshold the some of one hundred markes We will
and charge of Exchaqr ffr to out any proff a ofer charge to be be reprofand
thies o that thalbe your suffycient warrant and Discharge in that behalf be these presentes
Yet at o Citie of London the xxv daye of June the one and twentye yere of our Reigne

163

The autograph of John Bridges, clerk of the Tents and Revels, this hand is characteristic of the midcentury in its size and boldness, its heavy shading, its swashing descenders, and its ts strongly bent to the right.

After my right hartie comendacions, wheare as
therle of huntyngdon is apoyntyd generall beyonde
the Sees, The Counsailles pleasur is that he
be Furnyshid of Tentes of the kinges, that
is A Rounde howse with A hale, ketchin / offices   5
& lodging for his men, And that, forasmoche as
ther is not to serve his torne of olde howsis, in
store, but A kechin, that ye cause newe
to be made owt of hande with as moche spede
as maye be possible / of suche the kinges canvas   10
as remaynyth in store in your Custody; For the
which together with the Charges of other stuff and
workmanshipe I will gete the Counsailles
waraunt for you from the Courte this
xiiijth of Septembr 1549 /   15

          Your Loving Frende
          Arundell

5 *hale*] a pavilion or hut.
7 *howsis*] The *i* is the downstroke connected with the curved head of the *s*; this form of *i* after *s* will be met with elsewhere in these examples, sometimes undotted.

10 *canvas*] Because of a blot the second *a* is uncertain.

After my right hartie comendacons, wheare as
Castle of Huntyngdon is apoynted gyenall beyond
the Seas, The Counsells plesure is that he
be furnysshid of Tentes of the kinge, that
is a Round howse wth a hale, beyng offici
& lodging for his men, And that forasmoche as
this is not to have his tent of olde howses, in
stoare, but [it] beyng, that ye cause newe
to be made out of suche wab moche serue
as maye be possible, of suche the kinges cause
as remaynyth in stoare in yor Custody, ffor the
wch togethr wth the Charge of oth stuff and
workmanshipe I will gete the Counsells
warrant for your beyng the Counsell this
[x]th of September 1549/

yor Lobyng frend

The loyalty of Sir Thomas Cawarden, Master of the Revels, was suspected at the time of Wyatt's rebellion, 1554, and his armor was confiscated; this receipt was presumably issued to him at that time.

For sir Thomas Car'den knight

Cij. Corselettes at xxviij^s a pece amounting to   Cxlvij^{li} xvj^s /

C. Moryspikes at iij^s iiij^d a pece amounting to   xvj^{li} xiij^s iiij^d /   5

l. moryans with close eares at viij^s the pece amout   xx^{li} /   10

l. moryans with eares for hackbuttes at vj^s viij^d a pece amount   xvj^{li} xiij^s iiij^d /

xx^{ti}. stele collers at iij^s iiij^d a pece amount   iij^{li} vj^s viij^d /   15

xxij^{ti}. horsemans heddpeces at xiij^s iiij^d the pece amount   xiiij^{li} /

xx^{ti}. steale saddelles at xvj^s a pece amount   xviij^{li} /   20

xxx^{ti}. pair of gauntlettes at v^s a pair amou'   vij^{li} x^s /

vj. pair of vambraces with palderns at x^s a pece amount to   iij^{li} /

iiij^{or} velvett sadelles and a horseharneis of velvet amounting to   xxviij^{li} /   25

        Summa totalis   CClxxiiij^{li} xix^s iiij^d /

1 *Car'den*] The mark of omission is misplaced in Cawarden's name.

2 *Cij*] 102.

10 *amout*] This can be read either *amout* or *amont,* in either case an error.

14 It was a common though meaningless practice to write *ti* or *ty* or *tie* above *xx* for twenty; see also *xxx^{ti}* below.

17 *xxij^{ti}*] The scribe was thinking of "two-and-twenty"—a usage still to be heard in England.

25 *iiij^{or}*] On the same principle as *xx^{ti}*.

For Sr Thoms Sandow knyght

xij Corsletts at xxvj s a pece } xxiiij li xij s
amountyth to o——————————

v Moris pikes at iij s iiij d a pece } vij li xiij s iiij d
amountyng to o——————————

l moryans w ther caces at } xx li
xm s the pece amount o——————

l moryans w caces for harkbutts } xvij li xiij s iiij d
at vj s viij d a pece amount o————

xx Stele collers at iij s iiij d a pece } iij li vj s viij d
amount o——————————

xxvij horsemans held pece at xiij s iiij d } xviij
the pece amount o——————————

xx Stele saddell at xij s a pece amount o xij li
xxx pair of gantletts at v s a pair amo o vij li x s
xij pair of vambrace w paldrons at v s } iij li
a pece amount to o——————————

iiij velvet saddell and a horssharnes } xxvij li
of velvet amountyng to o——————

Sm totall o——————— vij xx xvij li xvij s iiij d

SIR WILLIAM CAVENDISH

LETTER TO SIR HUMPHREY BRADBORNE

AND THOMAS BABINGTON   [CA. 1555]

Only the signature and the line above it are Cavendish's autograph; the main hand has little of the characteristic appearance of the midcentury hands—largely because of the writer's restraint in his descenders. The right-leaning ts would, however, identify the period of the hand.

Right woorshipfull after my hartie commendacions theis shalbe
to let yow vnderstonde. Forasmoch as I am seased in one
parcell of grownd called medowplecke. The occupacion
wherof also I haue quyetly had by the space of twoo
or three yeres And so quyetly occupyenge the same   5
the xxiiijth day of this present monyth one henry Cryche
vnder what pretence I know not came into my said
grownd with dyvers mysdemeaned persons with hym / And
ther goinge to the mancion howse fownd my shepardes
wyfe with her chyldren in the said howse / which howse   10
they ryotuously and forceably entred into / And furth
of the same howse cast my said shepardes wyfe and
her chyldren And yet kepe the same with force
contrary to godes peace and the kinge and quenes as
by certen statutes wherof ye are not ignorant more   15
playnly dooth appeare / wherfore if it shall please
yow to see reformacion of such mysdemeanor commytted
contrary to the lawes I shall thinke my selfe moch
bownden vnto yow / Desyrynge your assystance no
further then the equytie of the mater will permyt   20
and the statutes in such cases haue provyded /

• • •

6 *present*] The *s,* with its unusually low head, is duplicated elsewhere in this letter, especially before *e* and *o;* it is a rare form but not peculiar to this writer.

13 *chyldren*] The *n* is blotted, but punctuation may have been intended.

14 *as*] The writer appears to have made the virgule and then written this word over it.

Right woorshipfull after my hartie comendacons this shalbe
to let yow understonde ffor as moch as I am seased in one
proll of growond called Medowplecke. The occupacon
wherof also I have quyetly had by the space of twoo
or three yeres And so quyetly occupyenge the same
the vem[th] day of this present month one henry Crosse
under what pretence I know not came into my said
growond and dyspoers my demeaned personn wth hym And
ther goinge to the mancon howse fownd my shepardes
wyfe wth her children in the said howse / wth howse
they ryotewsly and forcably entred into / And furth
of the same howse cast my said shepardes wyfe and
her children And yet kepe the same wth force
contrary to godes peace and the kinge and quenes as
by certen statutes wherof ye are not ignorant more
playnly doth appeare / wherfore iff it shall please
yow to se reformacon of such mysdemeanor comytted
contrary to the lawes I shall thinke my selfe moch
bownden unto yow / Desyrynge yo[ur] assystance no
furthher then the equytie of the mater woll permyt
and the statutes in such cases have provyded /
prayenge yow to let me know by this berer what
day and wher yow woll mete for the same / at w[ch]
tyme I woll attend uppon yow ther to declare such
mysdemeanors as are comytted This takyng my
leave I comytte yow to god / ffrom Chattesworthe
the vem[th] day off August

yo[ur] lovyng ffrende to comaund
Willm Cavendyssh

Though smaller, neater, and less exuberant than earlier examples, this hand is still characteristic of the midcentury, with its right- *bending ts and the thickness of the shaded strokes.*

For as much as, most worshipfull audience
herof latt all men haue done ther diligence,
in such honest myrth, as the time required,
and with great prayse achiued that we desired,
after matters most wittelye devysed,   5
and great labore most happely practysed,
we are come hither to troble yow as boyes.
and after sage thinges to shewe our trifflinge toyes.
Pleaseth hit yow therfore to be so favorable,
if we children make myrth as we ben able.   10
not desiringe prayse but to shewe ower witte,
in such exersise as for vs be fitte.
our vnablenes therin to take in good parte.
exceptinge the thinge for ower willinge harte.
and that in this yow may perceive our intent   15

I will shortly speke to yow the Argument.
On Chremes by Maud. his wiffe had iij children,
Wherof the on was a maid, and the other ij men.
of the ij the elder Iulye by his name,
loved greatlye his mothers maid Iulian.   20
and when that he had to her broken his mynd,
he found her to him in all pointes licke kind.
albehit his mother this well perceyved,
through wilkines devise she was so deceyved,
that she thought thone and thother from love as fre,   25
and as honest as any persounes mought be.
never thelesse afterward such chaunce be fell,
that Chremes to a marchaunt this mayd dyd sell.
but Iulies servaunt wilkin workinge such deceat,
Ioinynge Fenell to him in workinge his feat,   30

2 *herof latt*] *here of late.*
3 *myrth,*] Here and elsewhere in these two pages, a comma in the original manuscript is so pale and faint as not to show in the photograph.
8 *shewe*] The first *e* is uncertain, perhaps *o*; cf. the same word in line 11.
9 *hit*] *it*; a common spelling till well into the seventeenth century.

25 *thone and thother*] *the one and the other*; such elisions, particularly of the *e* in *the*, were common until at least 1700.
26 *persounes*] Could, of course, be read *personnes*, but this scribe favors *ou* elsewhere where *o* would be normal.

ffor as nowe as most worshipfull audience
hereof call all men have done their diligence
in theire honest myrth as the time requireth
and with great prayse assigned y[a]t not desired
after matters most worthelye devised
and great labour most earnestly practised
we are come hither to trouble yow as boyes
and after sage thinges to shewe y[e] triflinge toyes
please yt yow therfore to be so favorable
if we children make myrth as wee ben able
not desiringe prayse but to shewe owr will
in theire exercise as for woll be fitte
o[u]r enablenes therin to take in good parte
expectinge the thinge for owr willinge harte
and that in this yow may perceive o[ur] intent

I will shortly speke to yow the Argument
On Terences by mand his woffe had iij children
wherof the on was a maid, and the other ij men
of the iij y[e] elder hight by his name
loved greatlye his mothers maid Iulian
and when that he had to her broken his mynd,
he founde her to him in all pointes contrary kind
albeit his mothers this well perceyved,
throwinge wickines devise she was so deceived,
that she thought hone and hother fro love as fre,
and as honest as any personnes mongst be.
neverthelesse afterward suche channce be fell,
that Terences to a man's servant his mayd ded sell
but Iulius servant will in workinge suche deceat,
Joininge himsell to him in workinge his feat,

SIR GEORGE PIERREPOINT
AUTOGRAPH LETTER TO ELIZABETH, LADY ST. LOE 1561

A difficult specimen of the secretary hand, largely because of the crowding, the heavy inking, and the careless malformation of certain letters. There is in it a residue, not common so late as 1561, of older forms; the r, for example, in rewdlye (line 6) and in rathere (line 9) belongs to the bastard hand rather than to the secretary. The punctuation is merely whimsical. The addressee was the famous "Bess of Hardwick," whose fourth and last husband was George Talbot, sixth earl of Shrewsbury. Letters shown in Plates 10, 27, 30, and 50 are addressed to her, that in Plate 13 to her husband.

Right wurshipffull. and my verreye good ladye / after my
hertiest maner. I comende me to your good ladishipe / even so
preye yow. I meye be to good Mr Sentloo / most hertelye
thanckinge yow boothe / for your great paynes taken with me
at holme / acceptinge euerye thinge (thoughe it were neuer   5
so rewdlye handlyde) in suche gentill sorte as ye dyde
which doithe and will cause me to love yow the better whiell
I lyve / yf I were abill to doo yow othere pleassur or service
and the rathere because I vnderstand / that your ladishipe
hathe not forgotten my sowte to yow. at your goinge awaye   10
as speciallye to make mr sackvile & mr attorneye my
Frendes / in the matter betwene mr whalleye ande me
werin he doithe me playne wronge (as I take it in my
concyence) onelye to repe trouble & vnquyett me / but
I trust somoche in godes helpe / and partlye by your   15
ladishipes good meanes / and contynewance of your goodnes
towardes me / that he shall not ouerthrowe me in my rightiose
cause / and touchinge suche cominication. as was betwene
vs at holme / yf your ladishipe. & the gentillwoman your
doughtor lyke our boye vppon sight / aswell. as I & my wife   20
lyke the yonge gentillwoman / I will not shrincke one
worde. Frome that I said or promysed / by the grace of gode
who preserve your ladishipe / and my master your husbonde
longe togethere / in wealthe. healthe and prosperytie. to
his pleasure. and your gentill hertes desyer / Frome my   25
pover house at woodhouse. the iiijth of novembre 1561. by the
rewde hastie hande. of your goode ladishipes. assuredlye
allwaye to comaunde

George pierpounte.

2 *hertiest*] The final *t* is ill formed but intended; cf. *most*, line 3. *ladishipe*] This might be read *ladishepe*, but examination of other *p*s will show that what here looks like the loop of an *e* is in fact a part of the *p*.

5 *were*] The writer commonly elides *e* and *r*, as here.

7 *doithe*] *doth*; neither here nor in line 13 is this reading quite certain.

8 *pleassur*] The final syllable is contracted by the sign often used for *er* or *ur*.

10 *sowte*] *suit*.

11 *speciallye*] We can assume that the long tittle above was meant to indicate a contraction, though not a standard one. What Pierrepoint wrote was *spiallye*.

15 A space filler ends the line, not a letter.

Right worshipfull, and my vearaye good ladye, after my
hartiest manne I comende me to yo[ur] good ladishippe, even as
I praye &c. I maye be so good m[aste]r Carleton, moost hartelye
thankinge the bearer, for my greate paynes takin to ...
at Holme, except my one thinges ...
... doubte and will rem... me to lose of[f] the letter which
I lyke, yf I were able to do my ...
and the rather becaus I understand, that yo[ur] ladishippe
hath not forgotten my ... so ... at my comynge thorage
... so mak... ... ... m[aste]r attendinge my
frende, in the ... ...
... onlye to ... ... me, that
I first ... in yo[ur] ... and ... by yo[ur] ...
ladishipe yo[ur] ... ... of yo[ur] ...
forward me, that he ... ... in my ...
... and ... my ... remin ... as ... ...
... at Holme, yf yo[ur] ladishippe ... the gentillwoman yo[ur]
doughter, lyke as hir ... sister, as well as I & my ...
lyke the young gentillwoman, I will ... thinck one
who ... upon yo[ur] ladishipe, and ... yo[ur] ...
... ... in ... ... and ...
his pleasure, and yo[ur] gentill ... desire, ...
... by his hande. The xviij[th] of novembre 1561 by the
allwaye to comande. I yo[ur] good ladishippe, assuredlye

George Pierpoint K.

JAMES CROMPE

AUTOGRAPH LETTER TO ELIZABETH, LADY ST. LOE
[CA. 1565]

Though in the main secretary, this hand is contaminated by court-hand forms, notably the medial r and the h best illustrated in he in line 8. The use of numerous and exaggerated descenders and restrained ascenders is in part responsible for the unusual character of the hand. Crompe's habit of flatten-ing m, n, and i does not make for easy reading, and legibility is further reduced by an almost total want of punctuation, by some curious spellings and word forms, and by the dearth of initial capitals for names. Lack of space prevents the inclusion of the whole letter.

Mastur harry with wyllyames shall com vppe so sone as whe can
set them furthe he hathe no botes that wyll kepe owte water
so that there most be a peyre made for mr harrye abowte tewseday
he shalbe with you god wylling as tocheing mastur charles mastur
wyllyam cavendyshe seythe that yf you sent hym to tydsewall   5
all this larning that he nowe hathe shall do hym smalle plesure
for the skolemastur that he shulde goo to wyll teche hym aftur
anothur sorte so that he shall for gote thes techeinges wyche
he hathe had bothe at mr Iackeson teyler and wyllyames yf you
do meane to sent mr charles to ⟨x⟩ oxforde let hym not goo to   10
tydsewall/mr wyllyam cavendyshe had of late a lettur From
teyler from oxforde wherin he dyd wrytte that yf your ladyshippe
stode nede of a skolemastur he wyll com to you to chatteseworth
I shall staye charles for going to tydsewall tyll I knowe forthur
of your plesure mr w candyshe wyll se that he shall apleye   15
his boke tyll your plesure be knowon yf mr w/candyshe maye
he kepte were larning his he wyll be larnyd for he dothe stodye
& apleye his boke daye & nyght there nede none to call on hym
for going to his boke / I shall sent you all the moneye I
can gete chortely aftur Seynt tandrose daye your fatte   20

1 *Mastur*] An example of a superior final letter without abbreviation.
10 *to*] Crompe appears to have started to follow the *o* with an *x* for oxforde, and then to have deleted it without completion of the letter.
13 *stod*] The straight slanted line appears to have no function here.

16 *knowon*] The first *n* is written over another letter.
17 *were larning his*] *where learning is*
19 *moneye*] The final *e* could be read *s*.
20 *tandrose*] *Andrews*

mastar happy & wylliams shall com vppe so dom as we can

get the fyrst he saythe nobobes that wyll kepe owr watar

so that they must be agayne made for no happys abowte tero(?)

he shall wt yow god wyllyng as tochyng mastar gaskis mastar

wylliam cavendysshe sayth that yf yow set hym to tydyswall

all thys layng that he now sayth shall do hym smalle plesyr

for the scolemastar that he shuld goo to wyll take hym aftar

anothar boye so that he shall for doyt thys techyng wych

he sayth hath both at in Jacksons wyll & wylliams yf yow

do mane to sent no gaskis to oxford let hym not goo to

tydyswall no wylliam cavendysshe had of late a lettar ffs

wylls he oxford wych he doyt wyll that yf yor ladysshyp

stode mad of aftol... at he wyll com to yow to chattisworth

I shall stay gaskis for yory to tydyswall tyll I know fothar

of yor plesyr & cavendysshe wyll so that he shall aplys

hys boke tyll yor plessyr be knowen yf & cavendysshe may

be kept wey lang yf hys he wyll be layryd for he dothe stody

& aplys hys boke daye & nyght thys mans to call o hym

for yory to hys boke / I shall sent yow all the mony I

can do tho shortly aftar keptandos daye yor fathar

RALPH ADDERLEY

LETTER TO SIR NICHOLAS BAGNAL,

MARSHAL OF IRELAND 1567

The amanuensis who wrote this letter im- parts striking individuality to his rather attractive hand by the sweeping curved descenders, particularly those of the ys and some hs and the unusual crosses on his final lls and ffs.

After most harty commendacions Righte worshipfull evon So I Shalbe glad
to here of your yealthe and well doynges as your Brother Sir Rauff was
vppon Wensdaie last att Stafford castill and where as my Brother
in lawe the Brynger hereof Iohn Bagott haithe a vnconstant hedd
and is more youthfull and wilfull then Sober wittyd haithe vowed   5
a voyage into Ireland to go Sowe his wild ootes god Send them
good Reypinge / in dede he haithe witt ynoughe Butt a foole haithe
the kepynge therof / albeit I do assure you he is vnsusspected of
any vntruithe or oder notable cryme excepte a white lye) wiche is
taken for a Small fawte in thes partes / his Brother is a Sober   10
grave Ientilman of as good qualites and Bryngynge vppe and as
orderly doithe liff and the cuntrey aswell noble men as otheres haue
as good likynge and opynyon of hym as of any essquyer nott excedynge
CCC markes landes within iij Shyres where he dwellithe and that
your Brother Sir Rauff will affirme (nott fayntly) Butt withe Stearne   15
and yearnest wordes and cowntenaunce and for So moche as he haithe
no moo Brotheres butt this and lackithe the partes of acquyntaunce
and famyliarite withe you I make my Selff So Bold (of your
curtesy as to crave your frendshipe in this Said Beyreres behalff
and that it myghte pleyse you att this my instaunce nott only to   20
Bestowe your good advise and councell vppon hym Butt also to
helpe to place hym in Suche sorte as to your Wisdome shall Seme
good So that he maye be Stayed from Licencyus boldnes and the
Reign of libertie for feare he fall into owtragyus folly or wilfullnes to
the discomfort of his frendes if he did Susteigne Sume penurie or   25
Scaresnes vntill the Rage of youthe hadd Rune his Race I thyncke
hitt wold be a good chastesment vnto hym ⟨whose⟩ neuerthelesse his
            gouernement I do Referre
vnto your Wisdome and consideracion and in case he Staye in tyme
and growe to Sume conformytie and good order I will perswade withe
his Brother to be an ayde vnto hym and if otherwise he haithe   30
to moche alredy as god best knowithe whoo Send you yealthe
withe thencrease of moche worshipe this x of aprill. 1567

            youres assuredly (wherin he
                maye)   R Adderley

1 *Shalbe*] The initial has the form of a capital but seems to be intended as no more than an initial; still, because he also has a few minuscule initial *ss*, we retain the capitals. *B* we treat in the same way and for the same reason.
4 *haithe*] hath.
9 *(excepte*] The parenthesis ought to end after *partes* in the next line; Elizabethan writers in general exhibit a strange inability to get marks of parenthesis right, as can be seen again in lines 15 and 18.
25 *frendes*] Regularly used, as here, to mean one's immediate family.

After muste hartely comendacions Righte worshipfull even so I shalbe glad
to here of your healthe and well doynges as your brother Sr Rauff was
uppon wennsdaie last att Stafford castill and were as my brother
in lawe the Baynger knowes John Bagott haites a dwncostant hedd
and is more youthefull and wilfull then sober wyttyd haites vowed
a voyage into Ireland to go serve his will wch god send hym
good keppynge / in dede he haites witt ynoughe Butt a foole haites
les keppynge therof / albeit I do assure you he is vnsusspected of
any vntrewthe nor oder notable cryme (excepte a white lye) wife is
taken for a small faute in teis place his brother is a sober
grave gentilman of as good qualitees and Bayngynge uppe and as
orderly doinge lif and the curtesy aswell noble men as oder us have
as good likynge and opynyon of hym as of any of suche sorte accordynge
CCC markes landes wthin iij thinges were he dwellifes and teat
your brother Sr Rauff will affirme (nott foynth) Butt writes clearne
and agaynst wordes and countenannce and for so muche as he haites
no moo brothers butt teis and larkites teis pte of argumentacon
and famyliarite wittes you I make my selfe so bold of your
curtesy as to make your frendshipe in teis and Bayngers behalfe
and teat it myghte please you att teis my instannce nott only to
Bestowe your good advise and counsell uppon hym Butt also to
helpe to place hym in sure sorte asso your wisdome shall seme
good so teat he maye be stayed from liconyng boldnes and teis
reigne of libte for feare he fall into vntragynt folly or wilfulnes to
teis dscomfort of his frends if he did envterin omm penurie or
grevefnes vntill teis dayes of youthe have duune his stare I teorike
hitt wold be a good chastesin vnto hym and gowneu I do referne
vnto your wisdome and consideracon and in case he staye in hym
and grewe to onne conformytie and good order I will persuade wites
his Brother to be an ayde vnto hym and if oderwise he haites
to more about as you best knowites wee send you healthe
wites teomwalt of more worshipe teis C of Aprill 156

yours assuredly weerin he
shydom)

An excellent secretary hand written by a professional scribe. Here, as often, C and D are used initially in unimportant words, a fact which tempts the transcriber to reduce them to minuscules. But the minuscules of these letters are used initially as well as the *capitals; and this writer uses many other capital initials. The transcriber therefore has no logical choice but to retain all capitals as they are written. Several signatures are not shown.*

After our hartie commendacions / Vppon Complainte exhibited in the behalf of
Iohn De *Chauera* and other marchantes of St. Iohn De Luce, declaringe that
a Shippe of theirs named the Marye of St Vincent Loaden with Trayne, oyle,
& other marchandices, was spoiled at the Seas by one Capten Rokehavers, which
sithe the facte committed arrived & remayned at Sandwiche, there hathe byn   5
proces awarded by the Quenes Maiesties Commissioners of the Corte of
   Depredacions for
the recouerie of the saide goodes / and our Lettres sent for the due execucion
   of the same
And vppon that processe disobeyed & not answered according to the due corse
of the Lawes, the saide Commissioners haue for that contumacie graunted
   further
processe vnto the Complainantes / that a certeine Hulke with xij peces of
   ordenance   10
belonginge to the saide Capten Rockhavers, should be deliuered vnto them /
   For
executinge whereof we also addressed our Lettres as well to the Maior of Sandwiche, as to all other the Quenes Maiesties officers & Subiectes to whome it
apperteined, not withstandinge which proces, & our seuerall lettres as
   aforesaide / We
be eftesones informed by the complainte of the peticioners that they finde no   15
redresse towardes thexecucion of any of them, nor to the Recouerie of their
saide Losses, which we thinke to be verie inconvenient & not meete to be
   suffered
And therefore do requier & straitelie charge yow by these our Lettres, that yow
ether cause the saide processe to be served according to the trewe effect and
meanynge thereof, Or els to take straite order, that suche as withstande   20
or refuse to obeye the same maye appeare before the saide Commissioners
of the Corte of Depredacion to alledge the cause of their saide refusall
And thereof not to faile / And so we bidd yow farewell From St Iames
The Laste of Maye 1572.

         Your Lovinge freindes   25

N Bacon c[ustos] s[igilli]
  T Sussex
           R. Leycester:
           W. Burghley

5 *there*] This unusual *r* occurs several times later in the letter, along with at least three other kinds.

6 *Commissioners*] The only *m* that is written appears to have an extra minim, but since we find exactly the same thing in the same word in lines 9 and 21, we must look for another explanation; in fact it appears that the extra minim is the *i*.

After o[ur] hartie comendac[i]ons / vppon complainte exhibited in the behalf of
John de Chauera and other marchante[s] of S[ain]t John de Lure declaringe that
a shippe of theirs named the Mary of S[ain]t Vincent loaden w[i]th wyne, oyle
& other marchandise[s] was spoiled at the Seas by one Dauy Pokehardie, w[i]th
suche the parte comitted arryued & remayned at Sandwiche, there hath[e] byn
ordr[e] awarded by the Quenes Ma[jes]t[ie]s comyssioners of the Office of depredac[i]ons for
the restorie of the sayde goode[s], and o[u]r lr[e]s sent for the due execuc[i]on of the same
And vppon that ordr[e] disobeyed & not answered accordinge to the[e] dewe co[ur]se
of the lawes, the saide comyssioners haue for that contumacie grannted further
proces vnto the complainte[s] that a certeine hulke w[i]th co[r]n goode[s] of ordenance
belonginge to the saide Dauy Pokehardie shuld be deliuered vnto them, for
co[n]tentinge whereof we also addressed o[u]r lr[e]s aswell to the Mayor of Sand
wiche, as to all other the Quenes Ma[jes]t[ie] officers & subiecte[s] to whome it
apperteined, not w[i]thstandinge w[hi]ch proces, & o[u]r sewall lr[e]s as aforesaide, we
be eftsones informed by the complainte of the peticio[ne]rs that they finde no
redresse towarde the p[er]forma[n]c[e] of any of them, nor to the restorie of their
said losses, w[hi]ch we thinke to be borne inconuenient & not meete to be suffered
And therefore do requir[e] & straitelie charge yo[u] by these o[u]r lr[e]s, that yo[u]
either cause the saide proces to be obeyed accordinge to the trewe effect and
meanynge thereof, Or else to take straite ordr[e], that suche yo[u] w[i]thstande
& refuse to obeye the same maye appeare before the saide comyssioners
of the Office of Depredac[i]on to alledge the cause of their saide refusall
And thereof not to faile / And so we bidd yo[u] farewell / ffrom St. James
the Laste of Maye 1572.

yo[u]r Louinge ffrende[s]

T Sussex

R Leycester

W Burghley

This pure secretary hand has lost virtually all trace of what we have been calling mid-century characteristics. It is the work of a professional scribe who wrote fast and sometimes carelessly. Only the signature is in the earl's hand.

My verie good lord, because I haue now disposid ⟨for⟩ my
garrisons for this winter Season maynie gentlemen of my
companie are desirus to repose them selfes in England, some
for werines of those travells and hazardes that this Cuntrey
yeldith, other vppon better respectes as this bearer mr Candishe   5
who I assiur your Lordship hath in all seruices bene so redy and
willing to take paines as I cold not look for more of eny
privat or mercenary soldier, Therfore I cannot but giue
hym his due commendacion desiring your lordship and my lady to
accept of his retorne as of one licensid and commendid by me   10
And in very dead emonges all those that now leue this place
I know not one whose retorne shall be more acceptable
or for whome I can be better persuadid to do good /
Towching the seruices vndertaken here I leue to his report,
and ⟨of⟩ for the successe; I find more difficulty to traine the   15
gentelmen of our nacion to endure paines meet for soldiers, then
to bring to good effect the Iourney I haue in hand, wherin
I see no doubt at all, thoughe the begyning haue bene
somewhat vntoward. And so recommending the bearer
vnto your Lordship I bid you most hartely well to fare From   20
knockfergus the 23 of october 1573

Your Lordships assured frend
and kinsman
W Essex

6 *assiur*] A similar and undotted *i* may be seen in *desiring* (line 9) and similar but dotted *is* in *disposid* (line 1) and *desirus* (line 3); cf. also Plate 5, line 7, note.

14 *here*] This word cannot be read; it may be conjectured. The writer appears to have finished it off with several almost random movements of the pen. The first two letters are clear enough, and the last could be an *e*. The possibilities seem to be *here, heere,* and *herein* or *herin*. The first seems most likely considering the context; the second is hard to accept; the third or fourth make sense but do not look right, and the *is* are usually dotted.

My verie good Lord, forsmuch I have now disposed for my
garrisons for this winter ceasson, mayny gentlemen of my
compenie are desirous to repayre thaim selfe in England, shune
be wearied of thos travailes and hazarde that this winter
yeldith, other uppon better respecte as this bearer my standish
can I assure yor L. haye in all service bene so redy and
willing to take paynies as I vold not loke for more of my
speciall or ordenary soldiar, Therfore I cannot but geve
thaim this dew comendacion desiring yt yor L. and my lady to
haroept of thos esteme bee of our licensed and comendid by mee
she is very dead onsege be thos yat now come this place
I knew not one whose esteme shall be more acceptable
or be whome I may be better pshadid to do good
Towrching the former undertakers here I leve to this report,
and a for the suncesse, I fid more difficulty to trayne the
gentlemen of o maner to endure paynes meit for soldiers, then
to bryg to good effect the Journey I have n hand, wherin
I see no doubt at all, though the begynyng have bene
somewhat outward. And so comending the bearer
unto yor L. I bid yor most hartely, wale to fare this
Knockfergus the 22 of octob. 1573

yor L. assured frend
and kinsman.

INDENTURE OF RELEASE 1576

An indenture like the one shown here was often used for title deeds as a safeguard against malpractices. It was drawn up in duplicate, head to head on the same piece of parchment, and then cut in two with a wavy—indented—line. Each party to the deed signed and appended his seal to the copy that was to be kept by the other party.

This Indenture made the syxthe daie of Aprell in the Eighteneth yere of the Raigne
of owre soueringe Ladie Elizabeth bie the grace of god Quene of Englande Fraunce and
Irelande defendor of the Fayth. et cetera. Betwene Gabriell Pledall of Mudgehall within the parishe of
Lydiard Tregoose in the ⟨saide⟩ Countie of Wilteshire gentleman on the one partie And Syr Edwarde
Baynton of Bromham within the saide Countie Knighte on the other partie / Wytnesseth   5
that the said Gabryell Pledall for and in consideracion of certain somes of money to him
bye the sayde Syr Edwarde before thensealinge and delyuerie here of well and trewlie payde
Hathe releassed confirmed graunted bargayned and sold and bie these presentes dothe realeasse
confyrme graunte bargaine and sell, vnto the sayde Syr Edwarde Baynton all that his
righte title estate interreste terme of yeares and demaunde in and to one Pasture, grounde   10
or leaze with thappurtenances called Redbreache lyenge and beinge in the parisshe of Chippenham
within the countie aforesaide and nowe in the tenure and occupacion of William Norborne
yeoman, and in and to euerie parte and parcell thereof with thappurtenances what soever. To haue
And to holde the said pasture ground or leaze withall and singuler thappurtenances, to the saide
Syr Edwarde Baynton his heyers and assignes / to the onlie and proper vse of the saide   15
Syr Edwarde Baynton his heyers and assignes for euer In Wytnes whereof the
parties Fyrste aboue namede, Vnto these present Indentures Enterchaungeblie haue sett
their handes and Seales the daie and yeare firste aboue written

Gabriell Pleydell

2 *soueringe*] *sovereign.*
3 *Gabriell*] The bottom of the upside-down *r* sweeps back to join the first
part of the stroke of the same letter to give the appearance of an *a* following the *b*.

4 ⟨*saide*⟩] the spelling is uncertain. The word was interpolated and later
erased.
17 *Enterchaungeblie*] The last minim of *n* is obscured by the *g.*
18 *yeare*] Written over another word.

This Indenture made the [...] daie of Aprill in the Eighteneth yere of the raigne of oure Sonerayne Ladie Elizabeth by the grace of god Quene of England ffraunce and Irelande defender of the faythe &c: Betwene Gabriell Poole of [...] in the countie of [...] gentlemen on the one partie And Edmonde Baynton of Bromeham in the said countie Esquire on the other partie Witnesseth that the said Gabriell Poole for and in consideracion of a certaine somme of money to him by the said Edmonde Baynton before the ensealinge and delyuerie hereof well and truelie payed, hath [...] released confirmed granted bargayned and solde vnto the said Edmonde Baynton all that [...] one yerely grante bargayne and sale vnto the said Edmonde Baynton [...] all his estate interesse terme of yeres and demande [...] to vse [...] and to vse [...] in the [...] of [...] [...] in lease with [...] called [...] because he [...] bringe vnto [...] in the [...] [...] vnto the [...] and moue in the [...] and [...] and [...] [...] vnto the [...] with and to haue and holde [...] the said demysed premisses [...] vnto the said Edmonde Baynton his [...] [...] by these [...] [...] hereof [...] [...] And to haue [...] the said [...] [...] or assignes to the vses [...] Edmonde Baynton his heires and assignes to the vses [...] Edmonde Baynton [...] his heires [...] [...] In witnes [...] for his [...] [...] [...] to these presentes [...] [...] the yere [...] [...] aboue written

Robert [...]

by me Edward [...]

The large headings are in an engrossing hand, the text in a secretary that was a little old-fashioned by 1576, probably because of the provincial origin of the document.

The Inuentarye of all the
goodes and Chattells of Iohn Edolf late of
New Romnye gentleman deceased taken and
priced the xx.daie of Septembr 1576 in
the xviij.yere of the raigne of our soueraign
Ladye Quene Elisabeth.

In redie monye

Inprimis in his purse in redy monye   iiij^{li}
Item in monye besides the same   xx^{li}.

In Apparrell

Item fower gownes fower dubletes one ⎤
damask Cassok two paier of hose fower ⎬ x^{li}.
Shurtes two caps two hattes ⎦

In the haule.

Item two square tables two fourmes one ⎤
long Settle two chayers vj Cushions two ⎬ l^{s}.
Awndirons A fier fork A paier of tonges ⎥
and the hanginges about the same ⎦

The Inventarye of all the

goodes and chattells of John Dolf late of
New Romney gent Deceased, taken and
prised the xx daie of September 1576 in
the xxviij yere of the raigne of o[ur] sou[er]aign
Ladye Quene Elisab[eth]

In redie monye

Inprimis in his purse in redy monye   xl vj
Item in monye besides the same   s   xiij li

In Apparrell

Item fower gownes fower dubletts one
Damaske Casok two paiers of hose fower
Shurtes two capes two hatt   s   xx li

In the haule

Item two square tabbles two formes one
long settle two chayers v cusshions two
Andirons d fier pik d paier of tong s
and the hangings about the same   s   xls

Broughton, writing to the father of Anne Bagot, whom he is soon to marry (see Plate 20), employs his small, clear, excellent secretary hand for the first one-third of his letter and then switches abruptly (line 22) to italic. Perhaps he wanted to practice the latter, or perhaps he wanted to demonstrate his versatility as a penman.

Sir This bearer your seruant will sufficientlie signifie vnto you all
his travaill here, with the circumstances so that therein I will
not trouble you with any discourse /. but excuse his longer tarieng
then he was willinge vnto, by reason that in thend of this terme
both Mr Barroll and my self happened to haue more busines then   5
ordinarie, so that we had but startes to be furtherers /. and trust you
will hold him excused as one that is not long that cometh at lengthe.
aboutes the xviijth or xixth day of Iuly Mr Barroll and I accompanied
with two youthes my brethern entend to see you, and from thence to
thassises at Bridgnorth the xxjth of Iune. and to return to   10
see thassises at Staff[ord]. and from that day till the middes
of August I will remayne at my partners well likinge to make
her choise of tyme. from the myddes of August till michelmas
I thinke I shall haue occasion to make a progresse in South Wales
of easie lingringe iourneys / I haue sent to my partner a calendar   15
of my computacion of my prefixed busines, so that vpon viewe
thereof she may appoint the day /; to her best liking & yours. for
my self I am hers at half an houres warninge / whereas I wrote
to my cosin Newport to pay vnto your handes such money as remayned
in his hand to be conveied to London, because of my coming so   20
shortlie in to the countrey / I wishe you to stay it in your handes
if you haue rec[eiu]ed it. / or els my cosin to stay / I shall make sufficient
shift to serue my turn for a tyme. By reason of Busynes. I could
not haue leasure to go to the court to obtayne a Buck for your sonne
neuerthelesse I caused mr Baroll to make sute there, to mr treasourer   25
But he could not help. if my Busines will geue me leaue I will be at Court
on friday & trye my frindes./

• • •

8 *aboutes*] An old form of *about* which has survived in *hereabouts*.

10 *thassises*] The flourish with which he finishes off the *s* might be taken for an *e*; but *e* here is improbable for Broughton, whose spelling is never notably eccentric. The flourish occurs again in *michelmas* (line 13), where an *e* seems again unlikely, and in *partners* (line 12), where it seems impossible. On the other hand a similar final stroke in *coming* (line 20) could be an *e*, since Broughton does sometimes write *-inge*, but even here a meaningless flourish is on the whole more probable.

12 *partners*] In his later letters Broughton regularly calls his wife his partner, and she so speaks of him in hers. The word is not known to have been current in the sense of spouse.

17 *thereof*] The second *e* and the *o* appear to have been made with a curious counterclockwise loop.

25 *mr treasourer*] He would hardly have called the Lord Treasurer (Lord Burghley) "Mr. Treasurer," for the Elizabethans were particular about titles, yet any other treasurer would seem hardly to have been well enough known to be identified in this way.

This bearer yo[ur] s[er]v[an]t will sufficientlie enforme vnto yo[u] all
the travaile here, w[i]th the circumstance, so that therein I will
not trouble you w[i]th any discourse. but excuse the longer tarieng
here he was willinge vnto, by reason that in sted of their terme
both m[r] Darroll and our selfe hoped ____ to haue more leisure then
so it came so that we had but litle leysure here thevs[es] and trust you
will hold him excused. his one but is not long that cometh at lengthe.
aboute the ____ or overday of July m[r] Darroll and I accompanied
w[i]th ____ yonges my brotheren entend to see you, and from thence to
Chassier at Bridgnorthe the veraye same, and so retourn to
the Chassier at Staff. and from that day till the middes
of August I will remayne at my ____ well likinge to make
here reparell of tyme. from the myddes of August till mighelmas
I thinke I shall haue occasion to make a progresse in ____
of ____ lingeringe to index. I haue sent to my ____ a calendar
of my computacion of my ____ busines so that vpon distance
thereof he may appoint the day, to his best likinge ____ for
my self I am here at ____ in gode ____ ____ I wrot
to ____ in newport to ____ vnto your hand ____ mony ____ remayned
in his hand to be ____ to London, because of my coming to
____ in to the ____ countrey, I ____ you to ____ it in yo[ur] hand
till you haue ____ it. or else some ____ to ____ I shall make sufficient
____ to serue my turn for a tyme. By reason of busynes I could
not haue leasure to go to the court to obtayne a ____ for your sonne
neverthelesse I caused m[r] Daroll to make sute there, to m[r] treasorer
but he could not help. if my busines will geue me leaue I will be at court
on friday & trye my freindes. ____ my freind wolaston praieth me to
excuse him in that I haue caused all my partners sutes to be made
here. seing that your enstruccion was to haue part made in the
contrey. it is my fault if it be any fault I must confess, & if it be
not so aptly & fitly made I trust my partner will forgeue me
my offence. & for the charges of makinge w[hi]ch will be more
then ____ shall in the contrey, I challenge that as a thinge due for
my ____ who hitherto enclyned my self to small thrift or sauinge
nor do not meane at this instant to begynne, till hereafter my partner
shall persuade me thereunto & whatsoeuer exces is bestowed, I must take
the blame thereof. & for that litle that my freind wolaston hath guided for
my litle partner, m[ist]res Dorothy, & my charge, because I haue no thing worth the
bestowinge on them, in this my especiall tyme, I must requeut them to take
that of my small liberalitie. and for your money w[hi]ch you haue sent I doubt

The writer is experimenting with letter forms, especially in the first six or seven lines. The final s and the two rs in line 1 and the h of that (line 2) belong to the late-medieval bastard hand. He tries at least five kinds of r, of which that in purchacyng *was not successful and that in* preson *(line 6) is the ordinary secretary* r. *The* A *at the beginnings of lines 8, 12, and 18 appears to be merely eccentric. In the main the hand is perfectly ordinary secretary. One line of the original is omitted.*

A lesson for landbyers //.

He that wilbe wise in purchacyng
Muste observe thes Lessons folowing
Fyrste be suer, that all the Land clere be,
In title of Hym, that sellith yt to the.   5
Lykewise that he in noo preson Lye
And also of Perfitt mynd & memory
And that yt be not chargid one hower
With any tytle of Womens Dower.
Se whether the teanure be bond or free   10
Dyschargid eke twix feoffer and feoffe.
And that the Seller be of full Age
The Land likewise fre from any morgage.
Looke that the tayle thereof stand sound
and whether it be in statute bound   15
Consider what servis Longith thereto
and vnto whom the fre Rentes doth goo /
And if thow canst, in any wise
make thy Purchace euer with large warrantise:
vnto thyself: and thyn Heires also   20
For thus shuld a wise Purchaser doo /
Tho. Landbyers can not this Rule euer kepe
yet Shote at this marke, the Better to Spede

14 *tayle*] *entail.* *thereof*] The spelling is suggested by *thereto* (line 16).
20 *Heires*] The *i* is obscured by the descender of the *h* above.

22 *euer*] *always.*

A lesson for landbyers //

He that wille wisely purchase londe
Muste obsserve this lesson folowing
Firste be sure that all the Land clere be
for title of hym that selleth yt to the.
Lykewise that he in no possession be
And also of perfitt mynd & memory
And that yt be not chargid one howse
Nor any tytle of womens dowr
See whether the teanure be bond or free
Dyschargid eke twise statutes and feoffes
And that the seller be of full age
The Land likewise fre from any mortage
Looke that the taylonge of Land bynd
and whether it be in statute bound
Consider what thois longeth thereto
and unto whom the present doth too
And if thow canst in any wise
make thy purchat ew no warrantise:
unto thyself: and then shewe also
ffor thus shuld a wyse purchaser doo
The Landbyer can not this rule ew kepe
yett hete at this make the Bett to spede

A good example of a clear, neat secretary hand. Saunders always uses v in the initial position; medially his usual practice is like ours: v for consonant, u for vowel.

Good vncle, After my hartiest commendacions to yow and to mine aunt: It
    is not
vnknowen vnto yow what great heavines is happened to vs here at
welforde, & generallie to all our frendes besides, by the losse of my good
father mine onlie frende, & best staie, & greatest comfort in this worlde
whome it hath pleased God to call vnto his mercie. we are nowe by   5
this sorowfull accident becomme orphantes, fatherlesse & motherlesse, yet
I hope in this troublesome worlde God hath not left vs altogether
frendlesse or helplesse, in that he suffereth vs to enioye your life and
mine auntes, & the lives of other my deare & nere kinsfolkes which I beseeche ·
him longe to graunt for the mutuall comfortes of vs all, & I trust God   10
hath appointed it thus, partlie to this ende that my father beinge taken
from vs, wee should yet finde yow & mine aunt & others of our kinsfolkes
fast & suer frendes vnto vs, to succour vs and sticke vnto vs in all
cawses wherein we should neede your helpes & frendshippe, so farre as
right & equitie should requier. And for yow and mine Aunt, I do   15
assure my self as hetherto yow have ben frendlie & curteous towardes me, so
hereafter vppon occasion I may be bolde to crave and vse your frendshippes
and best helpes. I sende blackes to yow and mine aunt by this bearer,
as the necessitie of this heavie time requireth, they are not so good or fine
as yow are worthie of, or as my desier was to bestowe vppon yow, yet   20
I crave they may be accepted. the daie appointed for the solempnizinge
of the funerall is to morrowe sennight the xxth of this moneth, against
which daie I would desier yow & mine Aunt to be here. I have invited
my vncle dairell & mine Aunt, my Cosen Thomas dairell & his wife
my cosen Richarde Ingolsbie and his wife my cosen walter Bagott & his   25
wife, & my brother Tiringham, & do verelie looke for all their comminges
trustinge withall that yow & mine Aunt will not faile me. my Sister
Tiringham can not comme by reason that shee lieth in at this present, and is
latelie deliuered of a boie, God be praised that giueth vs somme comfort
amongest a great deale of sorrowe. This heavie newes hath ben kept   30
from her knowledge hetherto, & shall not by my consent be imparted vnto
her till suche time as shee be stronge againe.

                     • • •

6 *becomme*] The *mm* lacks a minim, but Saunders clearly intended to write *becomme*. Compare *comminges* in line 26.
18 *blackes*] mourning cloth

28 *comme*] In view of the writer's spelling of *becomme* (line 6) and *comminges* (line 26) we have to assume that his tittle over this word calls for a double *m*; see also *somme* in line 29.

7

Good vncle, After my hartiest comendacions to yow and to mine aunt: It is not
vnknowen vnto yow what great heavines is happened to vs here at
welford, e generallie to all our frende besides, by the losse of my good
father mine onlie staie, e best staie, e greatest refuge in this woeld
wgome it hath pleased God to call vnto his mercie. we are nowe by
this sorowfull accident become orphans, fatherlesse e motherlesse, yet
I hope in this troublesome woeld God hath not left vs altogether
frendlesse or helplesse, in that he suffereth vs to enioye yoʳ life and
mine aunte, e the lives of other my frende e neere kinsfolke wᵗ I besech
him longe to graunt for the comfortt of vs all, e I trust God
hath appointed it thus, yeelie to this ende that my father being taken
from vs, wee should yet finde yow e mine aunt e others of our kinsfolke
fast e sure frende vnto vs, to succour vs and sticke vnto vs in all
causes wherein we should nede yoʳ helpes e frendshippe, so farre as
right e equitie should require. And for yow and mine dueste, I do
assure my self as hetherto yow have ben frendlie e curteous towarde me, so
hereafter uppon occasion I may be bold to crave and vse yoʳ frendshippe
and best helpes. I sende blacke to yow and mine aunt by this bearer,
as the necessitie of this heavie time requireth, they are not so good or fine
as yow are worthie of, or as my desier was to bestowe uppon yow, yet
I trust they may be accepted. the daie appointed for the solemnizing
of the funerall is to morowe, viz the vᵗʰ of this monethe, against
wᵗ daie I would desier yow e mine Aunt to be here. I have invited
my vncle Cawell e mine Aunt, my Cosen Thomas Cawell e his wife
my coᵖ Bysard Ingolsbie and his wife, my coᵖ walter Bagott e his
wife, e my Brother Tiringham, e do verelie looke for all their cominge
trustinge wᵗʰall that yow e mine Aunt will not faile me. my Sister
Tiringham can not come by reason that she liethe in at this printe, and is
latelie delived of a boie, God be praised that giveth vs suche comfort
amongest a great deale of sorowe. This heavie newes hath ben kept
from her knowlege hitherto, e shall not by my consent be imparted vnto
her till suche time as she be stronger againe. I purposed to have bestowed
blacke uppon my vncle Beamont e my coᵖ Henry e his wife, e so to
have invited them hether but God hath disappointed me by shortninge of
my vncles daies, whome I praie God we may well followe when it
shall appoint the time, whereby it happenethe that my griefe is encreased
seeinge it was greater both then I was well able to sustaine, and that I
can not have my coᵖ Henrie Beamonte companie being nowe deiven
to comit blacke for himself e his kinsfolke e to make preparation for
my vncles funerall. Thus deare frende fall awaie, e sorowes are multiplied.
I praie yow comealt the funerall daie. welford house is but small of
receipt, e our companie wilbe great especiallie yf the daie be knowen.
So trustinge of yoʳ cominge e mine aunte and wishinge to yow bothe
as well as I am able I take my leave of yow mondaie the vᵗʰ of Julie
Ao Dni 1585.

yoʳ loving nephewe
william Edmunds.

Accounts similar to this one exist for dinners of the Star Chamber, the Privy Council, and other official bodies—always kept in this form and in this small, neat secretary hand. The fare was always either fish or meat.

A Dynner provided in the Treasourye chamber
for the Lord Treasourer the Barons and other
Officers of theschequire, sittinge there vppon hir
Maiesties affaires: the nynthe daie of December
in the xxxth yeare of hir highnes most prosperous Reign   5
Et Anno Domini 1587.

videlicet

Imprimis in breade viij^s in Beare vj^s in Ale
iij^s iiij^d. in Flower ij^s. in Lynge iij^s iiij^d.
in sweete butter viij^d. in salte salmon ij^s. in
Grenefishe xviij^d. in twoo gr[eat] pikes vj^s viij^d.   10
in two great Carpes vj^s viij^d. in two Capons
v^s iiij^d. in one great Tenche ij^s viij^d. in iiij.
Gurnardes vij^s vj^d. in vj. Whitinges vj^s. in
one syde and a Chine of freshe Salmon x^s.
in vj. Rochettes iij^s. in one great Codd. iij^s viij^d.   15
in di[midio] C. of Smeltes xx^d. in Crevishe x^d.
in one dozen Larkes xij^d. in Shrimpes vj^d in
pounde butter v^s. in Egges xij^d. in hearbes and
rootes for Sallettes xvj^d. in Fruicte vj^d. in
Biskettes and Car. iiij^d. in Sugar and all other   20
necessarie Spices x^s. in vineacre vergeous
musterd and onyons iiij^s in white salte di' b[ussello]
and bayesalte di' b[ussello] ij^s. In the Cookes wages
iiij^s. the buttlers wages xij^d. in Trenchers
xij^d. in rosewater vj^d. in barberryes vj^d.   25
in iiij pipkynns viij^d. in wasshinge of the
Naperye iij^s iiij^d. in wyne ij^s viij^d. in the
Skowrers Wages xij^d in the Porters wages
xij^d. in yeast vj^d. to the Turne spitt and twoo
other Labourers in the kitchin xij^d. in Fire
xij^s. in Portage vj^d. and in botehire xvj^d.

probatum
vj^{li} xviij^s vj^d.
per me. fra. guilpine

W Burghley   30

Wa: Mildmay

---

7 breade] The small looped mark following, which stands before each amount paid, was, in one form or another, customary.

16 di[midio] C.] half a hundred. Probatum] *approved*—by the auditor; the reading is conjectural, but some such formula was standard.

20 Car.] *Caraway* perhaps? In Shakespeare's 2 *Henry IV*, V.iii.3, Justice Shallow says, "We will eat a last year's pippin . . . with a dish of caraways."

22 di' bussello] *half a bushel.* The reading is conjectural.

26 iiij] Conjectural; the paper was damaged through folding.

Dynner provided in the Treasurye Chamber
for the L. Treasorer the Barons and other
Officers of the Exchequer, sittinge there uppon Her
Majesties affaires: the nynthe daie of December
in the xxx[?] yeare of Her Highnes most prosperous Reigne
Eliz Anno Dmi 1587

Imprmis in breade oviijs in Beare oijs in Ale
oijs iiijd. in Flower oijs. in Lynge oijs iiijd.
in sweete butter oiijd. in salte salmon ojs. in
Trenesishe oiijd. in twoo gr. pike ovjs vijd
in two great Carpes ovjs vijd. in two Tapones
ovjs iijd. in one great Tenche oijs vijd. in iij.
Turbardes ovjs vjd. in vj whitinges ovijs. in
one syde and a Chime of fresh Salmon o vs
in vj porgette oijs. in one great Gull oijs vijd
in DD. of Smeltt oviijd. in Irebishe o vd.
in one doz. Larkes oiijd. in Shrimpes ovjd. in
pounde butter o vjs. in Egge oiijd. in hearbes and
roobes for Salette oijd. in flrinks ovjd. in
Wistelle and Cav ovijd. in Sugar and all other
nessisarie Spices ojs. in Uineare Uergons &
musterd and onyones oijs. in white salte DD iijs
and bay salte DD iijs ojs. In the Cookes wages
ojs. the butlers wages oxijd. in Trenchers
oxijd. in rostwater oijd. in barberres oijd.
in riptinges oviijd. in washenge of the
Naprye oijs iiijd. in wyne oijs viijd. in the
Skowrers wages oxijd. in the porters wages
oxijd. in yeast oijd. to the Turne spitt and twoo
other Labourers in the kitchin oxijd. in flrire
oviijs in Portage oiijd. and in boteHere oxijd.

A round secretary, deriving much of its indi- *by an amanuensis who, when he remembered*
vidual character from the unusual swashing *to punctuate at all, threw in an all-purpose*
tails of h, x, y, and &. The letter was written *comma.*

Good father I haue sent by this carrier two suger loues they waegh
xxix pound and a quarter, which cometh to xxv^s vj^d & vj^d the bages
I haue sent therewith vj pounds of peper I bought of Mr Morly.ij^s vj^d
a pound, I haue bought mace he selleth it for x^s a pound, Cloues iiij^s
vj a pound when my mother needeth she shall haue some of mine, my   5
vncle Oker could help me with no more, I haue sent therewith a
gallan & a pint of sallet oyle which cost vj$^{s.}$ & iiij^d, I am verie glad to
heare that my sister Lettice shall come vp, my mother shall haue
her goune assone as I can get it made, my partoner is gone this day
to speake with Mr Dorrell about your accomptes, for vntill he haue bine   10
with the auditor he can not certify him of your accomptes, because
you had but a letter of Sir Amias Paulets and not an acquittance my
partoner telleth me that he will goe thorugh with it with asmuch speede
as he may, my brother Anthony is at Croidon where the Quene lieth
he saeth he deliuered your letter to Mr Grivvell & after went for   15
aunsweare & he told him that day he had written you an aunswear
by his man, I am sory that my vncle Ihon continueth in his old disordered
life, I sent you downe athinge from the high commissioners which wold
haue restrayned him, my partoner saieth that wold haue bine the
best course, he will not let his sonne weare a coate of penniston he   20
saith it is to whot he ⟨you⟩ caused me to ⟨by⟩ buy buffin for him Lil & Wat
which shalbe made vp with as little cost as I can, because you shall
see how the sicknes increaseth I haue sent you a bill of the last
week and this. So cravinge your dayly blessinge and my mothers
to me and my daughter I cease to troble you : Warw[ick] Inne this   25
xi of May

> Your obedient Daughter.
> Anne Broughton

13 *thorugh*] *u* is written over another letter.

15 *saeth*] The reading is not certain, the *e* being written, apparently, over another letter. See also *saieth* (line 19) and *saith* (line 21).

16 *aunswear*] The final *r* is defective and perhaps a final *e* is missing, because the writer's pen snagged on the edge of the paper (which does not show in the reproduction).

17 *vncle Ihon*] This is the man whom A. Adderley discusses at length in his letter (Number 11).

19 *wold*] The intended spelling cannot be determined; the writer seems to have written *woud* and then made an *l* on top of the *u*, but he may have done it the other way about.

21 *to whot*] too hot.

Good father I haue sent by this carrier two suger loues they waygh
vij pound & a quarter, which cometh to vij s & vij d & vij d the bagges
I haue sent therewith vj poundes of paper I bought of mr mowly ij s vij d
a pound, I haue bought mace he selleth it for viij s a pound, cloues iiij s
vj a pound when my mother needeth she shall haue some of mine, my
vncle Phox could help me with no more, I haue sent therewith a
gallan & a pint of sallet oyle which cost vj s . iiij d , I am verie glad to
heare that my sister Lettice shall come vp, my mother shall haue
her gowne assone as I can get it made, my partener is gone this day
to speake with mr Dowett about your accomptes. for vntill he haue bene
with the auditor he can not certifie him of your accomptes, because
you had but a letter of mr Amias Paulett and not an acquittance my
partener telleth me that he will goe thorough wth it with as much speede
as he may, my brother Anthony is at Croidon where the Queene lieth
he saith he deliuered your letter to mr Gwibbell & after went for
aunsweare & he told him that day he had written you an aunsweare
by his man, I am sorie that my vncle Ihon continueth in his old disordered
life, I sent you downe a thinge from the high comissioners which wold
haue restrayned him, my partener saith that wold haue bene the
best course he will not let his sonne weare a cote of pennistone he
saith it is to what then caused me to bi buy buffin for him Fil & coat
which shalbe made vp with as little cost as I can, because you shall
see how the prices increaseth I haue sent you a bill of the last
week and this. So wishinge youe daily blessinge one my mothers
to me and my daughter I ceasse to troble you . wards. Ime this
vi of may

                                              Your obedient Daughter.

                                              Anne Broughton

The reading of this hand will not prove so difficult as its general appearance perhaps suggests. Most of the letters are fairly well formed, though somewhat irregular. The size and appearance of the hand, both reminiscent of the hands of an earlier generation, suggest that the writer was a man of advanced years.

Iohne Owles I send you herin Inclosed
A byll of one goslynges wich wyll come to
you the seconde daye of the terme & paye
you lxx^{li} wich I praye you receyue of
hym & delyuer then his bonde to hym. this   5
berar also shall paye you twentie
pound wich vpon the receyte therof
delyuer hym A not of your hande. ⟨for⟩
therfore. Comende me to my cosen
your master & tell hym I am gladd   10
to gett money to gether to prove
out of dett. And god wyllynge
I hope to be   with hym in the
begynynge of the terme. And
yf yt plese hym to wryte to me   15
by this berar. I wolde be gladd
to her of his well doynge &: my
Ladis. And whether his viage
to see holdethe. Thus Indetted
to you for your paynes taken for   20
me I bydd you fare well Sprowston
this xx of Aprell your frende
     Myles Corbett

1 *Iohne*] The *n* has to be assumed though Corbett does not elsewhere so thoroughly flatten an *n* or *m*.
6 *berar*] *bearer,* the messenger.
8 *not*] *note.*
10 *master*] The correct reading may be *maister,* a common form, but an *a* marred by a slip of the pen or paper seems more probable.

13 The ink blot must have been made before *with* was written, since nothing was written under it.
15 *wryte*] The *r* written over what seems to be a *y.*
19 *see*] sea.
21 *Sprowston*] A parish and village in Norfolk and Corbett's seat.

Jhesus. I send you herein inclosed
a byll of one exchynge with right owne to
you the seconde daye of the somar & paye
you .CLxxx. nt I praye you woday of
hym & Colynder ther ful bonde thy. the
Colynder also fall paye you fowertie
pound, wich apon the wedyde thwich
Colynder fyn at not of your handr for
therfore. Comend me to my ofter
your master & tell hyr I am glad
to gett money to gether to proue
out of det. and god wyllyng
I hope to be ... with hyr in the
begynnyng of the terme. And
yf yt plese hyr to wryte to me
by thys berar. I wolde be glad
to her of her well doyng & my
ladis. And ... her mary
to her soldory. Thus indetted
to you for your paynut taken for
me I byd you fare well hyroneppe
thys ... yor frende
Myles Corbett

SIR NICHOLAS BACON

ADDRESS TO THE SERJEANTS-AT-LAW

DELIVERED IN 1559 [CA. 1590]

This specimen exhibits the regularity and clearness of the work of a professional scribe and, as a fair copy, lacks many of the abbreviations and contractions of this period.

An Exhortacion gyuen to
the Serieauntes when they were sworne
in the Chauncery in Anno domini 1559.
My maisters: vnderstanding (as I take my self to doe) your
wisedomes and honesties, I iudge that a fewe woordes shall suffyce to   5
put you in mynde of your offyces and dutyes. And leste I might seeme
to those that be here presente to be negligent in forgettinge my dutye
whiles I am carefull to remember you of yours, therfore I haue thought
goode according to the auntiente order noe lesse laudable than vsuall
to saye a woorde or two to you in this matter. I am sure yt is right   10
well vnderstande to you that the state and degree wherto yt hathe
pleased the Queenes maiesty nowe to call you is the highest and
greateste next my lordes the Iustyces that perteynes to the lawe.
And by the lawe (you knowe) euerye man enioyeth the Fruites pleasures
and commodyties of his goodes landes libertye and lief & that by yt   15
wholye.

14 *knowe*] The parenthesis mark and a curved descender of an *h* above are both mixed up with the *e*, itself a small ordinary *e* made without a pen-lift. The initial letter of the next word, *euerye*, has been mended, but what the error was cannot be made out.

16 *wholye*.] The period is an error, since the sentence continues on the next page.

The answeare by the Lord keeper

Given in the Queenes presence to the Lo. Mayor
when he was presented to her Maty Ao dni 1559

The Queenes Matie hath hearde and doth verie well understand yor
humble suit and petytion, and hath communicate the same vnto you that
her highnes thinketh that in this your elecion you haue done as wisedome
and consideracion wonld ye should and that she hopeth that this
wardes good gouernaunce shall make perfecte and euident prooffe therof
And therfore is content to approue yt and allow yt. And as by
this her allowaunce her higenes committeth to your Chardge vppon
yours suit the rule and order of her chieffe and principall Citty, soo
ys by your stely powre and commissons in the well executing in ann
of her higenes lawes and proclamacions, or in thadministracion of justice
to riche and poore indifferently for by your curarefull looking to
the conseruacion of commen ..., of her people, ann ill or disorder
should happen, her Matie mount to burthen you therwth, and to call
you to the answeart of yt. And therfore earnestlie requirette you
to do your office wth suche diligence and circumspection as you may
satisfie her higenes good hope and expectacion, and as neyther
her Matie shall haue cause to repente this her Admission, nor
you my Lord Mayor youre reioysinge of the Charge, nor your
brethren the Alldermen theyre elecion.

An Exhortacion given to

the Serieauntes when they were sworne
in the Chauncery in Ao. dni 1559.

My maisters, vnderstanding (as I take my self to doe) your
misdraues and honestie, I iudge that a fewe woordes shall suffyre to
put you in mynde of your offyces and dutyes. And lesse I might seeme
to those that be here presente to be negligent ni forgettyng my dutye
whiles I am carefull to remember you of yours, therfor I haue thought
goode accordinge to the ambitent order noe lesse laudable then vshall
to saye a woorde or two to you in this matter. I am sure yt is right
well vnderstande to you that the state and degree wherto yt hathe
pleased the Quenns Maty nowe to call you is the highest and
greatest next my Lords the Justyces that ploeng to the lawe.
And by the lawe you knowe euye man enioyeth the swete pleasures
and commodytios of his goode lande libertye and liffe (that by yt

weolye.

The body of the letter is in the rapid but clear and businesslike hand of an amanuensis. The signature, the complimentary close, *and the postscript are in Essex's autograph, an italic hand favored among the nobility.*

After my verie hartie Comendacions. I cannot write
severall lettres to all those that haue interest in the choyse
of the knightes of that Shere, to be apoynted for the Parliament
intended to be held verie shortlie: to which place I do
exceedinglie desire that my verie good frend Sir Christopher   5
Blount may be elected. I do therefore commend the matter
to your frendlie sollicitacion, praying you to move the gentlemen
my good frendes and yours in that Countie, particularlie in my
name, that they will geve their voices with hym for my sake,
assuring them that as they shall do it for one whome I hold   10
deare, and whose sufficiencie for the place is well knowen, to
them; so I will most thankfullie deserve towardes them, and
your selues any travell, favor or kyndenes that shall be showed therein.
Thus I committ you to godes good protection. From Hampton Court
the 2d of Ianuarye 1592/   15

your very assured frend.
Essex

I persuade myself thatt my
creditt is so good with my contrymen
as the vsing of my name in so   20
small a matter willbe enough to
effect yt. butt yete I pray yow vse me
so kindly in yt as I take no repulse

1 *Comendacions*] The curled flourish on the *s* is the mark of contraction, -*cons* for -*cions*.
4 *do*] This word illustrates two points: (1) the initial *d* that looks like a capital but is not intended as one; (2) the practice of attaching *o* to a preceding letter, usually in common, short words (cf. *to*, the last word in line 11).
6 Blount was Essex's stepfather.
23 This appeal was successful, but when Essex foolishly tried to get another friend chosen as the second knight of the shire he was repulsed.

After my verie hartie Comendations. I cannot write
severall lres to all those that have interest in the choyse
of the knighte of that Sheir, to be apoynted for the parliament
intended to be held verie shortlie: to wch place I do
exceedinglie desire that my verie good frend Sr Christofer
Blount may be elected. I do therefore comend the matter
to yor frendlie sollicitacion, praying you to move the gentlemen
my good frends, and yt in that Contrie particularlie in my
name, that they will geve their voice wth him for my sake
assuring them that as they shall do it for one who most I hold
deare, and whose sufficiencie for the place is well knowen, to
them; so I will most thankfullie deserve towardk them, and
yor selves any teavice, favor or kindenes that shall be shewed herein.
Thus I committ you to god good protection. From Hampton Courr
the 2 of Januarye 159⁴/₅

I persuade my selfe that my
credditt is so good wth my contrymen
as the using of my name in so
small a matter will be enough to
effect yt. butt yett I pray you vse me
so kindly in yt as I rate no repulse

your very assured frend.

E R

Broughton's smaller, earlier secretary hand is reproduced (with his early italic hand) in Plate 16. The present hand, firm, confident, and controlled, represents the secretary almost at its best. Scarcely a letter in it is less than perfectly clear. Here is exemplified a common Elizabethan custom of placing punctuation marks well below the line.

Good Brother, with fowle way and faire wether we came the
first night to Newport, the second night to Shrewsbury
third home, and Robin was lively all the way, but my partners
horse stumbled in the foule way an Abbay Foryet that the
horse was downe on his brest and Peckt my partner, but   5
I thanke god she eskaped great danger, but she is not
so well to ride with me to Ludlow, whither she is the lother
to go, for that she will not go from Robin, by reason I
haue not bene at Ludlowe, where I am to receaue money
due for attendance, I cannot send to you by this bearer as   10
I would, but you shall shortlie heare from me, and thus
with 1597. comendacions from my partner and my suster with thankes for our
good Cheare, and not forgetting Nant Letyce, with blessing to Mall
nephewes Lewis harvie and dicke and Nan, with our humble dutie
to my mother we committ you to god this saterday. 17. December   15
      Ich Braud.
      Rich Broughton

5 *Peckt*] *To peck* usually means, of a horse, to stumble, but here, apparently, to throw the rider.

12 *1597. commendacions*] Broughton's eccentric way of dating letters.

13 *Nant*] *Nant* or *naunt* was a familiar form of *aunt* (from *mine aunt*). Lettice Bagot, Broughton's sister-in-law, had been called Naunt Lettice from early childhood.

16 *Ich Braud*] Slightly corrupt Welsh for *Your brother*. Broughton lived on the Welsh border and was of Welsh ancestry.

Good Brother wth foule way and fayre wether wee came the
first nyght to Newport, the second nyght to Shrewsbury
and home, and Robin was lively all the way, but my father
horse stumbled in the foule way in Abbay foryet that the
horse was downe on his brest and welsh my father, but
I thanke god he escaped great danger, but he is not
so well to ryde wth him to Ludlow whither he is the lother
to go, for that he will not go from Robin, by reason I
have not bene at Ludlow, where I am to receive money
due for attendance, I cannot send to you by this beare as
I would, but you shall horthe heare from me, and thus
wth 1597 comendacons from my father and my sister wth thanke for o
good chere, and not forgetting mant ... wth blessing to Mall
... my mother wee comitt you to god this saterday. 17. Decr

Jch Braud.

Rich Broughton

WILLIAM CECIL, LORD BURGHLEY
LETTER TO MATTHEW HUTTON,
ARCHBISHOP OF YORK   1597

This letter, in the hand of an amanuensis, is hastily written but not really hard to read. One can, after getting the feel of it, quite easily read the words and follow the sense. Being certain of the spelling of every word is another matter, because the writer often simply fails to form individual letters. In exactly the same way many writers of the present day indicate certain elements of a word by a mere wavy line or even a straight line, relying on context to identify the word. Only a few examples are pointed out in the footnotes; the reader may wish to work the others out for himself. The postscript is in Burghley's italic autograph.

After my vearie hartie Commendacions, to your G[race]
and the rest. I haue receiued your lettres written the
xijth of this monethe mentioninge the apprehencion of one
Ioseph Constable, a brother of Sir Henry Constables, with
sum others with him, beinge as it semeth common Receiuors   5
of Seminaries, and such leke bad persons, movinge
mee by the same your letter to direct yowe mine opinion
in what corse, and with what speed yowe showld proceade
against the said Constable: whearein I cannot direct
yowe anie thinge, but must leaue the same to your selves: 10
Onelie I haue thowght good to lett yowe vnderstand,
that vppon the dowbt conceiued by your Mr Ferne, of
the validitie of his Inditement, I haue in the absence
of the Iudges required the opinion of hir Maiesties Attorney
generall, whose awnsweare yowe shall perceiue by   15
his lettre to mee, which I doe send heareinclosed to yowe
with the Copie of his Inditement, by which yowe will
finde the same to be erronious: and wheare yowe
require to vnderstand mine opinion for his sendinge
vpp, I see noe such cawse to haue him to be sent   20
hither./And so I bid your G[race] and the rest
hartelie farewell./ From my howse in the
strand this xixth of Marche. 1596.
       Your G. assured Lovinge frend. /
your gr[aces] lettre to me   25
shewyng your desyre and opinion   W Burghley
for a presid[ent] hath bene greatly
lyked by hir Maiesty for your syncere
advise/

1 *G*] This capital letter is not so strange as it may appear. The *G* in line 24 is closer to the normal shape of this kind of *G*.

2 *lettres*] The abbreviated form in the MS, *lres*, is a common, almost a universal contraction for this word. For an understanding of the shape of the contraction as it stands in line 2, a look at *selves* (line 10) will be helpful, for the *-es* ending is made in the same way but more clearly. Then the *e* in *anie* (line 10) and the final *s* in *erronious* (line 18) can be seen to be similar to the final letters of *selves* and *lres*.

8 *yowe*] The contraction in the MS must mean *yowe* (see line 11). In lines 15, 16, and 17 it means the same. But in lines 12 and 21 the same contraction has to mean *your*. We are forced to assume that the scribe thought of that squiggle as being the proper ending for either *your* or *yowe*, when contracted.

After my harty thankes Commendations, to yo{u}r L:
and the rest. I haue receaued yo{u}r l{ett}re written the
xvij{th} of this moneth: mentioninge the apprehension of one
Joseph Constable, a brother of S{ir} Henry Constables, who
him selfe w{i}th him, being as it semely common Bandiers
of Seminaries, and suche like bad persons, moninge
vnto be the same y{a}t L{ett}re to direct yo{u}r owne opinions
in regard: w{hi}ch, and w{i}th regard that yo{u} should procede
againste the s{ai}d Constable: whearein I cannot direct
yo{u} anie thinge, but most commit the same to yo{u}r selues:
Onelie I haue thought good to lett yo{u} vnderstand,
that vpon the doubte remoued by yo{u}r M{aster} Sherine, of
the validitie of S{ir} Indictem{en}t, I haue in the absence
of the Judges required the opinion of S{ir} mashd M. Sng{e}r
generalle, whose answeare yo{u} shale perceaue by
his l{ett}re to mee, w{hi}ch I doo send herewithenclosed to yo{u}
w{i}th the Copie of S{ir} Indictements, by w{hi}ch yo{u} will
finde the same to be erronious. And wheare yo{u} are
required to vnderstand mine opinion for the proceadinge
w{i}th, I can not thinke cause to haue him L: be put
either. And so I bid yo{u}r L: and the rest r
hartelie farewell. From my howse in the
Strand the xixth of marche. 1596.

yo{u}r L: assured louinge frend,

W Burghley

yours g{o}o{d} l{ett}re to me
sheweth yo{u}r desire and opinion
for a p{ri}sd hath bene greatly
liked by hir M{aiesti}e for yo{u}r sincere
aduise

A pure secretary hand. This scribe's hs, with very low heads and low-sweeping descenders, would, in the absence of other evidence, suggest a date not much before 1600.

The Examynacion of Hugh Foorde of Harford in
the Countye of Devon husbondman taken by Iohn
Hele Serieaunt att Lawe and Thomas Hele Esquire
on the xviijth of Aprill. 1598 /
The said Hughe Foorde Confesseth that on Frydaye   5
last he tooke a sheepe owte of Roberte Barons Fold
which was his owne as he sayeth / and being asked
what is become of the Fell thereof/aunswereth
he knoweth not, nor whether he had or bought the
same Sheepe / he also confesses that he hathe   10
none of his own /

        Io Hele
        Thomas Hele

5 *Confesseth*] This initial need not be regarded as a capital (see introduction, page 13), but in view of the minuscule *c* in line 10 and the scribe's erratic use of capital initials, *C* here seems correct.

8 *aunswereth*] An *s* is obviously intended, but it is, strictly, an *f*.

Under the above title a version of this work was printed in 1629 and was soon after attributed to Francis Bacon. The heading below is in an "engrossing hand," often used for titles and the like, and imitating "black letter" print. The secretary hand is contaminated only by a few italic hs.

In what thinges the use of
the Lawe consisteth
The vse of the Lawe consisteth principally in theis two thinges
Thone to secure mens persons from death and violence
And thother to dispose the property of Landes and goodes.   [peace   5
For safetie of persons the Lawe provideth that any man   Surety of the
standinge in feare of another may take his oath before A
Iustice of Peace, that hee standeth in feare, and then the
Iustice shall compell the other to bee bound with Suerties to
keepe the Peace.   10

57

The Examynacon of Thomas Sharde of Harford in
the Countye of Deon Husband taken by John
Hele Esquire att Lawe and Thomas Hole Esquire
on the xxvth of Aprill 1598

The said Thomas Sharde confesseth, that on ffryday
last he tooke a sheepe out of Robte Barons flock
wch was his owne at the fayre, and being asked
w^hat is become of the ffell therof, answereth
he knoweth not, nor whether he led or brought the
said sheepe, he also confesseth that he stoale
none of his owne.

Jo Hele

Thomas Hole

In what thinges the vse of
the Lawe consisteth

The vse of the Lawe consisteth principally in theis two thinges

Thone to secure mens persons from death, and violence
And thother to dispose the property of Landes and goodes.

For safetie of persons the Lawe provideth, that any man   Surety of ye peace
standinge in feare of another may take his oath before A
Justice of ye peace, that hee standeth in feare, and then the
Justice shall compell the other to bee bound with Sureties to
keepe the peace.

SIR CHARLES CAVENDISH

AUTOGRAPH LETTER TO HIS MOTHER, ELIZABETH

TALBOT, COUNTESS OF SHREWSBURY [CA. 1600]

The hand represents an advanced stage in the transition from secretary to italic. The consistent use of the italic e is at so early a date unusual in a transition hand. Only the d and the k here always retain their pure secretary forms. The c is sometimes secretary (conference, line 2; perceaues, line 5) The v and w are close to secretary. Other letters are essentially italic. The es contraction (frendes, line 10) is out of place in the italic hand, and the swooping descenders give to the whole a vaguely secretary appearance. The end of the letter is not shown.

My humble duty rememberd./ this daye I was at Mr Dales
and my brother William with me who had conference with the
ould gentelwoman and she sayes that she vtterly mistook Mr
Talbott when he reported your Ladyships offers for she thought it
had bin doble as much as now she perceaues it is but not   5
withstandynge she sayes she doubtes not but your Ladyship will deall
well if the matter take effeckt but gladly she would haue
that your Ladyship ⟨w⟩ did com vpe for she and ⟨s⟩ hir husbande
had rather agree in consent with your Ladyship then talk ⟨with⟩
by any frendes./ agayne she hath promised hir Magesty   10
not to conclutt any maryage with out makinge hir priuy
vnto it soe that for that espetiall cause she wisheth
your Ladyships presence for that she thinketh your Ladyship
fittest and best able to attayne it sonest./

. . .

My humble duty remembred. This daye I was at Mr Dales
and my brother William w{th} me who had conference w{th} the
onld gentelwoman and she sayes that she vtterly mistooke Mr
Talbott when he reported your La. offers for she thought it
had bin doble as much as now she perceaues it is but not
w{th}standynge she sayes she doubtes not but your La. will deall
well if the matter take effect but gladly she would haue
that your La. w{ch} did com vse for she and hir husbande
had rather agree in consent w{th} your La. then talk to
be any frend. agayne she hath promised hir Magesty
not to concludt any marryage w{th}out makinge hir privy
vnto it soe that for that espetiall cause she wisheth
your La. presence for that she thinketh your La.
fittest and best able to attayne it sonest. my brother
bought a Iuell and presented it in your La. name, but
humble thankes was giuen vnto your La. but the mayd
would receaue non w{th}out hir mothers consent, then hir mother
was toold how your La. had sent hir
daughter a token and wished that she myght weare it
as a well wyshing from your La. and that your
ment not to receaue it agayne nether to bind hir to
any inconuenience by the receatt of it, the thankes
was giuen but she would not admitt hir daughter to
take it w{th} thes words that vntill some further sowtany
would not receaue any thinge

An official directive written in a clear and easily read hand. The place names and signatures are in italic.

After our verie hartie commendacions; It is much against her Maiesties most gratious mynde to laie such burthen of charges on her good and loving Subiectes as these tymes of late haue required; but being drawen thereto by
necessitie for the honor and safetie of her State, and fyndeinge the affaires
of Irelande in such tearmes at this present as some encrease of her Forces   5
there to the number of 2000. foote and 100. horse maie with Godes favoure
ether vtterlie represse or (at the least) verie much beate downe the pride
and power of the Rebelles by the end of this Sommer; It pleaseth her
Maiestie in her wisedome to thincke it much more convenient (as in deede it is)
for the leavyinge of the said smale nomber of horse to vse the helpe   10
of some fewe gentlemen of best abilitie and such as are of spetiall note
for theire good mynde and forwardnes to doe her service, then to make it a
common charge to the countrie; To which purpose whereas her Maiestie
hath likewise bin pleased to make spetiall choise of so manie gentlemen
by name as maie suffice for this smale supplie (in which nomber your selfe   15
are one) and by her lettres vnto vs vnder her owne hande to giue vs com-
maundment by our lettres to signifie her pleasure in that behalfe vnto euerie one
of them; yow are not here vppon to conceaue that her Maiestie hath made choise
of yow rather then of others to beare parte of this charge for anie disfavoure
toward yow whereby she might take occasion to burthen yow, but rather for   20
the confidence she hath in yow, and good opinion of your willinge mynde to
doe her service; Whereof as she is pleased to make vse vppon this
vrgent cause for her service, so she will retaine a favorable remembrance
for your good as occasion maie serue; We doe therefore hereby lett yow
vnderstande that her Maiesties pleasure is to require of yow one light horse   25
well furnished with a carasse, a light horsemans Staffe of verie good
lengthe, One Pistoll, and espetiallie a good Sworde, and withall a fitt
and able man to serue on the same, to be at *Chester* by the .25. of Iuly
next from thence to passe into Irelande, which man and horse yow shall but
lend vnto her Maiesties service, because it is intended that at the end of this   30
Action now to be vndertaken both the one and the other (God willing) shalbe
retorned vnto yow, and in the meane while shall haue good entertainement
of her Maiestie to beginne assoone as they shalbe at *Chester*; And so we
bidd yow hartelie farewell. From the court at *Greenewich* the 29
of Iune 1600   35

Your verie loving freendes. /

Tho. Egerton	C[ustos] S[igilli]	T Buchurst	Notingham
G Hunsdon	Ro: North		
W. Knollys	Ro: Cecyll	IFortescu	

1 *is*] Here the writer forms the *s* with a hooked attacking-stroke, as he often does, but not always; when, as in line 30, he writes *is* with an undotted *i*, it could be mistaken for *es*.

10 *smale*] In this word the writer shows clearly how he formed his *a*.

15 *suffice*] The writer did not cross the first *f*.

26 *horsemans*] The *e* has collided with the last stroke of the *s*. Compare *horse* in line 25.

28 *.25.*] The *5* was written over another numeral, and, lest it should not be quite clear, the writer repeated the *.25.* in the margin (not photographed).

30 *the*] Part of the *e* was smudged.

After o[ur] verie hartie Com[m]endac[i]ons; It is much against her Ma[jes]tie most gratious mynde to laie sure burthen of Charges on her good and loving Sub=
iectes for these tymes of late that required; but being drawen herto by necessitie for the hono[ur] and safetie of her estate, and findinge the affaires of Ireland in such tearmes at this p[rese]nt as some encrease of her forces there to the nomber of 2000 foote and 100 horse maie w[i]th [?] good favour there utterlie represse or (at the least) verie much beate downe the pride and power of the Rebelles by the end of this Somer, It pleaseth her Ma[jes]tie in her wisdome to thincke it much more Convenient (w[i]th m[u]che adoe etc) for the leavyinge of the said smale nomber of horse to take the helpe of some fewe gentlemen of best abilitie and suersall[?] are of speciall note for theire good mynde and forwardnes to doe her service, then to make it a Com[m]on Charge to the Countrie; To w[hi]che purpose w[e] are as her Ma[jes]tie selfe, likewise bui[?] pleased to make speciall choise of some gentlemen by name as maie suffice for this smale supplie (in w[hi]ch nomber yo[ur] selfe are one) and by her lettre sente you under her owne hand to give us Com[m]andem[en]t by yo[ur] lettre to signifie her pleasure in that behalf sente unto one of them; yo[u] are not herevpon to conceive that her Ma[jes]tie selfe maie de[v]ise of yo[u] rather then of othe[rs] to beare parte of this Charge for anie disfavoure towardes yo[u] whereby shee might take occasion to burthen yo[u], but rather for the confidence shee hathe in yo[u] and good opinion of yo[ur] willing mynde to doe her service; she hereof as shee is pleased to make note vpon this p[rese]nt Cause for her service, so shee will retaine a favorable remembrance for yo[ur] good as occasion maie serve; We doe therefore hereby lett yo[u] vnderstand that her Ma[jes]tie pleasure is to require of yo[u] one light horse well furnished w[i]th a Carbine, a light gentlemans staffe of verie good lengthe, one Pistoll, and especiallie a good Sworde, and w[i]th all a fitt and able man to serve on the same, to be at Chester by the 2[d?] of July next from thence to passe into Ireland, w[hi]ch man and horse yo[u] shall but send vnto her Ma[jes]tie service because it is intended that at the end of this Action, now to be vndertaken bothe the one and the other (God willing) shalbe returned vnto yo[u], and in the meane while shall thave good entertainement of her Ma[jes]tie to beginne assone as they shalbe at Chester; And so we bidd yo[u] hartelie farewell. From the Court at Greenew[i]che the 29
of June 1600

yo[ur] verie loving freindes:

Tho. Egerton   [Buckhurst]   [Nottingham]

G Hunsdon   Ro. North

[illegible signatures]

The letter appears to be about the last illness of Queen Elizabeth. The hand is pure italic except for the use of a secretary e now and then. It is unusual at so early a date to find such consistent use of the round s as Cecil's; only once (occasion, line 12) does *he make a tall s apart from double s, for which he follows the usual practice of using one tall and one short. Sir Robert Cecil, later earl of Salisbury, was the great Lord Burghley's second son.*

Mr Lieutenant you know It is a tender
thing to censoure the lyfes of Princes
much more of our deare soverain
but to honest men all things are
safe, and to my freends I am not   5
politick. To conclude my opinion (be-
syds my hope) is certainly that she will
recouer this sickness, for she doth
evry day more feele her sickness
and her dulness vanisheth which was   10
the only great signe of danger /
you shall heare from me as occasion
serves and ever find me as I haue
told you confident in
the Inocensy of my hart   Your louing   15
and in the honest zeales   freend
of a good Patriot and

                                    Ro: Cecyll

1 *you know*] There can be no certainty as to how one ought to construe the two identical final letters; *will* (line 7) and *was* (line 10) give warrant for *know,* while in line 12 we have to read *you* rather than *yow,* and it seems improbable that a man whose spelling in general is so regular and modern as Cecil's is would adopt so old-fashioned a spelling of a common word and even more improbable that he would spell it in two ways. We simply have to accept the fact that he was careless in the formation of his letters when he was writing fast.

3 *of*] Compare with this curious *o* the one in *to* (line 5).

12 *from me*] The strange mark between these words is the dot over the *i* in *find;* cf. *sickness* (line 9).

Mr Lieutenant you know It is a tender
thing to censure ye lyfes of Princes
much more of our deare Soveraine
but to honest men all things are
safe, and to my freends I am not
politick. To conclude my opinion (be:
sydes my hope) is certainly yt shee will
recover this sickness, for shee dotz
evry day more feele her sickness,
and her dulness vanisheth wch was
ye only great signe of danger
you shall heare from me as occasion
serves and ever find me as I have
tyld you confident in ye
ye Innocency of my sort (Your lovinng
and in ye honest zeale   freend
of a good Patriot and

Lovelace

HENRY CAVENDISH

AUTOGRAPH LETTER TO HIS MOTHER,

THE COUNTESS DOWAGER OF SHREWSBURY 1605

A simple, restrained, and almost childish-looking example of the secretary hand, *unusually clear and easy to read. Lack of space prevents inclusion of the signature.*

Ryght Honorable, with owr most humble and dutyfull
thankes, for your Ladyships bountyfull goodnes towardes vs at all
tymes, my Wyfe and I haue made boulde to present
your Honorable good Ladyship, with shuch poore and homely thynges, for
a symple newyears gyfte, as thys place can aford beshe-   5
chyng that accordynge to your Ladyships accustomed goodnes,
you wyll vouchsafe them in good part; and we shall
praye most earnestly to God almyghtty, to send your Honorable
Ladyship, many happy and healfull new years. And so
humbly cravyng your Ladyships dayly blessyng to vs both,   10
We most humbly take owr leave.
                    Tutbery the last of Decem. 1605
                        Your Ladyships humble and
                            obedyent soonne.

2 *Ladyships*] The writer's consistent practice of placing a dot high above the line after his abbreviations *La* and *Ho* can only be thought a personal eccentricity. Presumably the dots have the value of the usual periods used by other writers.

Ryght Honorable, Wt ovr most humble and dutyfull
thankes, for your La bountyfull goodnes toward vs at all
tymes, my wyfe and I haue made boulde to present
your Ho: good La; wt such poore and homely thynges, for
a symple newyeares gyfte, as thys place ca aford, besse=
chyng that accordynge to your La accustomed goodnes,
you wyll vouchesafe them in good part; and we shall
praye most earnestly to God almyghty, to send your Ho
La; many happy and healfull new yeares. And so
humbly cravyng your La dayly blessyng to vs both,
Wee most humbly take ovr leaue.
Cuthbery the last of Decem: 1605.

your La humble and
obedyent sonne.

The distinctive secretary hand (of Francis Bacon's half-brother) is marred by slovenliness in the formation of many of his letters and words, and he does not differentiate appreciably between some capitals and the minuscule form—notably the hs. This leaves it to the transcriber in each case to guess at Bacon's intention and then proceed to make an arbitrary choice.

The Examination of Stephen Nicholls of Ivore
in Buckinghamsheire taken the daie and
yeare aforesaid.

He saith that his age is about xxvj^{ty}, and that he hath bene
brought vp to drawe, and as a Scrivener, and was some 5
tymes a scholler in Oxforde. And is now setled in Eley
wher he hath made his abode for this halfe yeare paste.
And before his comminge to Eley had his abode at London in
Goldinge lane, wher he kepte shop as a drawer for the
space of a yeare, And hath bene married to one Hogges 10
daughter of ware, two yeares sone after midsomer laste
He sayth that he came from Eley to be placed in this Countrye
to teach a schole, And beinge asked why he brought his
wife with him, aunswereth, that she came to see him setled
He saith that he hath no acquaintance in thes partes about Hempton 15
but about Newton bridge he hath.
He saith that he was never in Harforde Gaole as a prisoner
He saith at walsingham faire laste he fell in to the companie of
Henry Hopkins who brought him ther acquainted with severall
of the Countrye here in Norff[olk]. And that Hopkins tould him of a 20
great lyvinge was fallne vnto him.
He saith that he came to the gaole at Hertforde, but to see Hopkins.
but vpon better advisement, he saith that he was indited, comminge
in vpon bayle, and was ther at Harforde acquitt about two
yeares since, And was called in question for a robbery done 25
vpon the high waie.
He saith, that when he was at Hempton faire yesterdaie he was
not acquainted with anie ther, but Edward Nicholson, Henry Hopkins
and one warde, that came out of Suff[olk].

Na: Bacon 30

4 *xxvi*^{ty}] *six and twenty.*
12 *Countrye*] An indeterminate area where a
man lives and is known.

13 *asked*] the *d* is written over a *y*.
15 *Hempton*] The *e* is deformed but can be inferred from line 27.

The Examinacion of Stephen Nirgetts of Frome
in Barckinge geuen before taken vj Idio dnm
yeare aforesaid

He saith that his lyue is about xxviij, and that he was borne
brought vp to drawe, and as a Caruier, and was some
tymes a Styller in Oxforde. And is nowe settled in Ely
wher he saith made his abode for this halfe yeare paste.
And before his remouige to Ely had his abode at London in
Golding lane, wher he kepte shop as a drawer for the
space of a yeare. And hath beene married to one Hogges
daughter of roane, two yeares sowe after midsomer laste.
He saith that he came from Ely to be placed in u ys cuntrye
to beare ye styller, And beinge asked wher he brought his
wife w¹ him, hee aunsweres, that she came to see him sethen
He saith that he hath no acquaintance in uys partes about Hampton
but about Newton bridge he saith.

He saith that he was neuer in Herforde Gaole as a prisoner
He saith at michaelmas was firme laste he fell into ye companie of
Henry Hopkins wch brought him into acquainted w¹ seuerall
of ye cuntrye gere in Norff. And that Hopkins tould him of a
treat huomage woud fallen vnto him.

He saith that he came to ye gaole at Herforde, but to see Hopkins
but vpon better advisement. He saith that yt was mislihed, to mige
w¹ vpon bayle, and nows yet at Herforde lyinge about two
yeares firme. And nows railled in question for a robbery done.
vpon yt his he woue.

He saith, that when he was at Hampton fami y sherdaue he was
not acquainted w¹ anie gre, but to Enward Nirgolson, Henry Hopkins
and one roone, that came out of Suff.

Na: Bacon

PRIVY COUNCIL
LETTER TO SIR ARTHUR CHICHESTER,
LORD DEPUTY OF IRELAND 1607

Because of its slant and the nearly complete absence of sweeping descenders (becoming old fashioned by 1607), this hand has a rather modern look. Still it is almost pure secretary, apart from the proper names, including October, all of which are in an italic hand.

After our verye hartye commendations vnto your Lordship. Vppon
sute made vnto his Maiestie for leaue to be granted vnto Sir
Randol Mc.Donnel to come ouer, wherin as ther
is no cause knowne here, for which his desyer should
be hindred; so we haue bene commanded to let your Lordship   5
vnderstande that his Maiestie is gratiously pleased
that you should graunte vnto him a lycense for
so longe tyme as you shall thinke fitt. And
so we bid your Lordship hartely farewell. From the
court at *Whythall* this last of *october* 1607   10

Your Lordships verye lovinge frendes

[Elle]smere Cancellarius   T Dorset   Notingham   T Suffolke

E. Worcester   HNorthampton   Salisbury

IFortescu   I Herbert   Iul. Caesar

1 *Lordship*] What letter the clerk had in mind when he wrote the small superior letter, it is impossible to say. It does not look like *p*, for Lordshi*p*; *l* is out because the addressee is singular; we are forced to settle for *s*, standing for *ship*.

12 When the Archbishop of Canterbury was present he signed in this first position; otherwise the Lord Chancellor did.

14 *IFortescu*] Sir John Fortescu always, as here, made a monogram out of his first initial and the ff of Fortescu. *Iul. Caesar*] Sir Julius Caesar, son of an Italian physician and immigrant to England, was born Julius Caesar Adelmare but later dropped the surname.

After o(ur) verye hartye commendations vnto yo(ur) L(ordship). vppon
sute made vnto his Ma(ties) for liaue to be graunted vnto S(i)r
Randol Mc Donnel to come ouer, wheerin as theere
is no daunt knowne heere, soe wo(uld) his desyre shoul(d)
be hindred; So wee haue bene commaunded to let yo(ur) L(ordship)
vnderstande that his Ma(tie) is gratiously pleased
that yo(u) shoul(d) graunte vnto him a lycence for
so longe tyme as yo(u) shall thinke fitt. And
so wee bid yo(ur) L(ordship) hartely farewell. From the
Court at Whytehall this last of October 1607

Yo(ur) Lo(rdships) verye & lovinge freindes

Ellesmere-Canc   T Dorset   Notingham   Suffolke

E Worcester   H Northampton   Salisbury

Stanhope   Ro Herbert   Jul Cæsar

As a general rule, if a writer habitually used capital C and D, but not other capitals, initially in adjectives, verbs, etc., as well as in nouns, it is reasonable to assume that he was not thinking of these as capitals but merely as initials, and therefore to reduce *them to minuscules in transcription. Here, however, the writer not only uses capital C and D, but seems to use other capitals quite indiscriminately, and we therefore retain all capitals. Only a small part of the inventory is shown.*

In my Ladys Chamber.

Item vj peeces of tapestery hanginges of Imagery

Item a Feelde-beadstid the toppe & vallance imbrodered
  with the Kinges Armes, v Curtines of Crimsen.

taffata sarsnett Lind with bayes & nett worke   5

the toppe Linde with nett worke/

Item a Downe beade & boulster. a fine wolle
  quilte & a Corse. Downe pillowes — iiij

Item a Crimsen Rogge.

Item iij greate square Coshines of Imagery   10

Item one Littell. Coshen/

Item a Cheare & ij stowles of Ierishe stiche
  with Cavers. to them of greene Cotten

Item a Lowe yealowe velett Cheare.

Item ij foote Carpittes   15

Item a littell table Carpett of nedle worke

Item iij blew Carpettes of brode Clothe

Item a walnott tree table with in Layd worke

Item a Longe Coshen of Collerd silckes/

Item a Table with Leaues.   20

Item a Corte Coberte

Item a Littell table with a frame

Item a wicker Cheare Linde with Read Clothe

Item a skreene of blew Clothe with a frame

Item a travis of pentadose with a Rode to it   25

Item a paire of Awnd Iernes fier shovell
   & tonges & bellous.

8 *Corse*] The reading is not clear, perhaps *Corser*.

10 *iij*] The *i* appears to be written over a *v*.

13 *Cavers*] The writer must have meant *Covers*, but he wrote *Cavers*.

25 *pentadose*] In later inventories of the same household goods this word is several times spelled *pentadus*; it is otherwise unknown but must be the kind of cloth the traverse is made of.

In my Ladys Chamber.

Itm vij peeces of tapestry (hangings of Imagery)
Itm a feelde bedstidthe toppe pallance imbroddered
wth the Kinges Armes, to curtines of Crimson
taffata fasnett Lind wth bayes & nett worke
the toppe Lind wth nett worke

Itm a downe beade & boulster a fine wolle
quilte & a chest, downe pillowes — iij

Itm a Crimson rugge.

Itm iiij great square Cushins of Imagery
Itm one Litell Cushen

Itm a cupbord ij stooles of frindg fringe
wth cappes to them of greene Cotten

Itm a Longe yealowe velet cheare.

Itm ij foote Carpittes

Itm a litell table Carpett of nedle worke
Itm iij blew Carpettes of brode Clothe
Itm a walnott tree table wth in Layd worke
Itm a Longe Cushen of Cullerd silkes
Itm a Table wth Leaves
Itm a Corte cubbert
Itm a Litell table wth a frame
Itm a wicker Cheare Lind wth Red Clothe
Itm a skreene of blew Clothe wth a frame
Itm a trapit of hangadose wth a Rode to it
Itm a paire of Andeirons fire shovell
& tonges & bellous.

LETTICE KYNNERSLEY

AUTOGRAPH LETTER TO HER BROTHER,

WALTER BAGOT [CA. 1615]

A species of italic hand often practiced by women. This lady (to give her the title she would have expected) spells less erratically than many did, and her punctuation is *usually sensible, if not according to any rule. Very little transcription here will enable anyone to read it with ease.*

Good brother my husband doeth erenestley intreat you. to doo so much
for him: as send for my cosen Pettie. and pay him this :5^l:
which you shall receue bie this bearer. and I pray you. will
him to make anote vnder his hand. what he hath receued: I
thank him he is willing to receue it bie :20^l:at aday till :80^l: 5
be run up: and so I hope my husband will be able to pay it.

• • •

Good brother my husband dothe ernestley intrente you. to doo so much
for him: as send for my cosen Pettie. and pay him this :5:
which you shall resue bie this bearer. and I pray you. will
him to make a note vnder his hand. what he hath resued: I
thanck him he is willing to resue it bie:20: at many til:80:
be run vp: and so I hope my husband will be able to pay it.
the first paymyent of twenti pound. be geueth at sent Iamestite:
he had thought to haue com him selfe. but for his trobelsome neghe
bors: good brother will you do somuch for me. as be ernest with
my fother in law. that he wold be freinds with my husband
for if he had but his contenance: he might goe thorow with
them. a grente deale better: wee haue much round of=
fered vs. and my husband goes in danger of his life: euery day
and I haue bin afrayde the wold pull downe the house ouer
my heade: for the haue nether the feare of god. nor of any
lawes: I pray you remember my dutie to my good mother:
this with my kindest comment to you. and my good sister
wishing you all happines: I rest your louing sister euer

Letise Kinnerslie

At first sight this hand might seem to have been written about the time of the original letter. But the restrained and controlled ascenders and descenders, though they are occasionally found much earlier, are more characteristic of the first decades of the seventeenth century. The hand is clearly, carefully, and legibly written, and is not a difficult one to read. Only the opening of the letter is shown.

Sir Fraunces Drake his letter to
Mr Iohn Foxe./.
Mr Foxe, whereas we had of late happie Successe
against the Spaniardes, I doe assure my self that you
have happely remembred vs in youre good prayers, And   5
therfore I have not forgotten brieflye to make you pertaker
therof. The .19. daye of Aprile .1587. we arryved within
the Roade of *Cales*: where we found much shippinge./
But emongst the rest .32. of verie great burthen, laden
& to be laden with provision: and prepared to furnish the   10
kinges Navie, intendinge with all speede against England;
The which (when we had boorded & also furnished our
severall shippes with provision as we thought sufficient)
we burnt. And althoughe by the space of two dayes &
two nightes that we contynued there, we were still in daunger   15
bothe with the thundringe shott from the towne, & assaulted
with the roaringe Cannons of .12. Gallies: yet we sunck
two of them, and one great Argosie, & still anoyed them
with verie small hurt to our selves. And so at our departure,
we brought away .4. shippes of provision to the greate   20
terror of our enemyes, & honor to our selues: as it might
appeare by a most curteous letter wrytten vnto me with a
Flagge of Truce by *Don Pedro* Generall of the Gallies./
• • •

8 *Cales*] Cadiz.

Sr ffraunces Drake his letter to
Mr John ffoxe. 1.

Mr ffoxe, whereas we had off late happie successe ~
against the Spaniardes, I doe assure my selfe that you
have hartely remembred vs in your good prayers. And
therfore I have not forgotten brieflye to make you pertaker
therof. The .19. daye off Aprill. 1587. we arryved within
the Roade off Cales: where we founde many shippinges. /
But amongst the rest. 32. off verie great burthen, laden
& to be laden wth provision: and prepared to furnish the
kinges Navie, intendinge wth all speede against England;
The wch (when we had boorded & also furnished owr
severall shippes wth provision as we thoughte sufficient)
we burnt. And althoughe by the space off two dayes &
two nightes yt we contynued there, we were still in daunger
bothe wth the thundringe shott from the towne, & assaulted
wth the roaringe Cannons off .12. Gallies: yet we sunck &
two off them, and one great Argosie, & still annoyed them
wth verie small hurt to owr selves. And so at o departure,
we broughte away. 4. shippes off provision to the greate
terrer off owr enemyes, & honor to owr selves: as it might
appeare by a most curteous letter wrytten vnto me wth a
flagge off Truce by Don Pedro Generall off the Gallies. /
But whereas it is most certaine, that the kinge dothe not
onlie make speedie preparation in Spayne, but likewyse ex-
pecteth a verie great fleete from the Straightes, & diverse
other placed, wch shonld Joyne wth his forces to invade England:
We purpose to set aparte all feare off Daunger, and by
Gods sufferance to proceede by all good meanes
we can devyse to prevent theire cominge. / Wherfore I
shall desyer you to contynue yor faithfull remembrance

WILLIAM WILSON
AUTOGRAPH LETTER TO EDWARD ALLEYN [CA. 1617]

Difficulty in reading this hand is due to the impossibility of distinguishing some of the es from some of the is. The transcriber can only look for guidance, in each crux that he meets, in the writer's spelling practices where these can be discovered. The close of the letter is omitted because of the shortage of space.

Right Worshipfull my humble dutie remembred
hoping in the Almighte of your health & prosperety
which on my knees I beseeche him longe to contynew /
For the many favors which I haue from tyme
to tyme receaved my poore abillety is not in the   5
least degree able to give you satisfaccion onlie
as I and myne haue byn bounden to yow for
your many kyndnes soe will wee duringe life
pray for your prosperety. I confesse I haue
found you my cheifest frend in midest of   10
my extremeties which makes me loath to
presse or request your favor any further yet
for that I am to be married on Sonday
nexte—& your kindnes may be a great
helpe & furtherance vnto me towardes the   15
raisinge of my poore & deiected estate I
am enforced once agayne to entreat yow ⟨nowe⟩
worshippes furtherance in a charitable request which
is that I may haue your worshippes Letter to mr
Dowton & mr Edward Iuby to be a meanes   20
that the Company of players of the Fortune
maie either offer at my wedding at St Saviours
church or of their owne good natures bestowe
somthinge vppon me on that day And as ever
I and myne will not only rest bounden vnto   25
yow but contynewally pray for your worshippes health

1 *humble dutie*] Here the similarity of *e* and *i* is clearly shown.

5 *abillety*] Warrant for the spelling is furnished by *prosperety* (line 2) and *extemeties* (line 11).

6 *give*] The curious *e*, which occurs again in *wee* (line 8), is inexplicable.

16 *raisinge*] The *in* is written over the downward stroke of the *s* and *e*.

17 *yow*] When deleting *nowe* Wilson forgot to change the *yow* to your.

Right wor[shipfull] my humble dutie is remembred —
Hoping in the almightie of y[ou]r health & prosperitie
which on my knees I beseech him long to continue,
ffor the many favor[s] w[hi]ch I have from tyme
to tyme received my poore abillitie is not in the
least degree able to give you satissfacion on lie
as I and myne have byn bounden to yo[u] for
yo[u]r many kindnes she will w[i]ll during my life
pray for yo[u]r prosperitie. I confesse I have
found you my ... friend in midest of
my extremities w[hi]ch makes me loath to —
presse or request ... favor any further yet
for that I am to be married on Sunday
next — yo[u]r kindnes may be a great
helpe & furtherance unto me toward the
raising of my poore & ... estate I
am enforced once agayne to intreat yo[u]r ...
and furtherance in a charitable request w[hi]ch
is that I may have ... a ... letter to mr
Dowton & mr Edward ... to be a meanes
that the company of players of the ffortune
may either ... at my wedding at ...
... or of their own good natures bestowe
... upon me on that day. And as ever
I and myne will not only rest bounden unto
... But continually pray for yo[u]r ...

A bold secretary hand rather old-fashioned by 1619, with its powerful descenders and strong loops. The strongly spurred a and the spurred c in Talmache (line 1) and Buck (line 6) are survivals not often seen at so late a date. We might reasonably assume that the writer was not a very young man.

Good Sir Lionell Talmache.
This bearer Mr Gosnold his
Maiesties gentleman vsher. goeinge home
to make merie with his frendes in the
Cuntrie. hath desired me to bestowe   5
a Buck of him. and my self
haveinge noe Comaund there. nor
knowinge any of whom I may
more boldly intreat that Curtesie .
than your self. I have thought good   10
to make it a request vnto you,
desireinge you to doe me the kindnes
to bestowe one vpon him out of your
parke at Helmingham. And I
will not faile in the like or any   15
greate request you shall make
to me. And will rest.
   Court at Woodstock
   this 26th of August   Your very assured
           1619,   lovinge frend & kinsman   20
                    Pembroke

2 *bearer*] The two different *r*s are both of frequent occurrence in this letter; for the first, which is anomalous, cf. *desired* (line 5), *Curtesie* (line 9), *request* (line 11).

Good Sr Lionell Talmadge
This bearer Mr Goffould his
M^ts gentlemen usher, goeinge home
to make merie with his frende in the
Contrie, hath desired me to bestowe
a Buck off him, and my selfe
showinge two Contened theire, nor
knowinge any of whom I might
more boldly intreat, yet betake
upon myselfe, I have thought good
to make it a request unto you,
desireinge you to doe me the kindnes
to bestowe one upo him out of yor
parke at Helmingham. And I
will not faile in the like or any
greater request you shall make
to me. And will rest

Court at woodstock
this 26th of August
1619

Yo^r very assured
lovinge frend & kinsman

[signature]

Otley

On the subject matter of this letter by a student at Oxford, see the Introduction, page 9. The hand, though essentially secretary, exhibits a reduction in the exaggerated ascenders and descenders and so shows the writer to be a child of the seventeenth century. He wrote a transitional hand reflecting the growing preference for simplicity and clarity which was effecting the gradual shift from the secretary to the italic hand. Young Bagot indicates the nature as well as the direction of the shift by his use of the italic tall s, made head first (but see also the secretary form in molest, *line 8, and* rest, *line 11). The turn away from the characteristically medieval use of abbreviation and contraction is also well illustrated here.*

Deare./

Father) I haue receaued your kind, and fatherly letter: kinde in that there-
by you aduertise me of thinges necessarie for maintinance which I was to
      receaue,
and according to your letter haue receaued; fatherly in that you by a fatherly
admonition command a reformation of a thinge amisse, to witt, the forme
      of my   5
writing, which if I had knowen before I coulde easily⟨e⟩ haue altered, and
      hence
forth will daylie showe that I can easily change it, nether will I there by any
more showe a barren invention. Thus feareing lest with my prolixitie I may
      molest⟨,⟩
your more serious cogitations, or incurre your displeasure, giueing you
      hartie thankes
for that I haue at this time receaued, & with the rememberance of my humble   10
dutie vnto you, I humblie take my leaue, and rest.

Oxon: the 22th
of Aprill. 1622:/

                    your dutifull and obedient
                    sonne. William Bagot./

3 *thinges*] The *g* is written over another letter.
receaue] Bagot tinkered with the *u*.
6 *easily⟨e⟩ haue altered*] Standardization of spelling was under way before 1622, but it had not proceeded very far or had much noticeable impact on most writers. It is remarkable, there-fore, to find a young man making two such corrections as Bagot makes here. Many a writer well after 1622 would have thought either *easilye* or *altred* quite satisfactory, even if we assume that they would have noticed the spelling at all.

Deare S

(father) I haue receaued your kind, and fatherly letter: kinde in that there:
by you aduertise me of thinges necessarie for maintinance wch I was to receaue,
and according to your letter haue receaued; fatherly in that you by a fatherly
admonition command a reformation of a thinge amisse, to witt; the forme of my
writing, wch if I had knowen before I coulde easily haue altred, and hence
forth will daylie showe that I can easily change it, neither will I hereby any
more showe a barren invention. Thus fearing lest wth my prolixitie I may molest
your more serious cogitations, or incurre your displeasure, giuing you hartie thankes
for that I haue at this time receaued, & wth the rememberance of my humble
dutie vnto you, I humblie take my leaue, and rest.

Oxon: the 22th
of Aprill. 1622

Your dutifull and obedient
sonne William Bygot

The passage is extracted from a manuscript version of the two parts of the play, cut and combined into one play, for private performance at Surrenden, Kent, the seat of Sir Edward Dering, bart., by amateur actors. It is the earliest surviving manuscript of any of Shakespeare's plays. The hand is, except for stage-directions and speakers' names, pure secretary. The punctuation, though eccen-tric and somewhat erratic, is not senseless. Like many other writers of the time, the scribe who copied this dramatic piece uses a form of capital C simply as initial c, and he does the same with capital A. Since these capitals have no significance and since other initials are in the main minuscules, we do not preserve, in the transcript, C and A.

Enter Falstalff.

Prin:, No if rightly taken: halter: here comes leane
   Iacke: here comes bare-bone: how now my sweet
   creature of bombast: how long ist agoe Iack:
   scince thow sawest thine owne knee: 5
Fals:,—My owne knee: when I was about thie yeares
   (Hall) I was not an eagles talent in the
   waste: I could haue crept into any aldermans
   thumb-ring: a plague of sighing and greefe
   it blowes a man vp like a bladder: there's   10
   villanous news a broad: here was Sir Iohn ⟨B⟩
   Braby from yowr father: yow must goe to the
   court in the Morning: the same mad fellowe
   of the North: Percey: and he of wales
   that gaue Amamon the Bastinado: and made   15
   Lucifer cuckhold: and swore the diuell his
   true liedgman: vpon the crosse of a
   welsh hooke: what a plague call yo⟨ ⟩w
Poyn:, Owen Glendower: hime
Fals:, Owen. Owen: the same and his sonne in   20
   lawe Mortimer: and old Northumberland
   and the sprigh[t]ly Scot of Scotts: dowglas
   that runnes a horse-backe vp a hill
   perpendicular:

4 *Iack:*] The trimming of the leaves by a binder appears to have cropped off the upper point of the colon, which on this assumption is here restored.

10 *there's*] Though he misplaced it, we may assume that the writer intended the apos-trophe to go in the right place. The modern use of the apostrophe in contractions of this sort begins to be met with in the first decades of the seventeenth century.

19 *Owen*] The *w* is written over an *o*.

Enter Falstaff.

Prin: No it is mightily taken: halter: heere comes leane
Iacke: heere comes bare-bone: how now my sweet
Creature off bombast: how long ist Ager Hal
since thou sawest thine owne knee.

Fals: My owne knee: when I was about thie yeares
(Hall) I was not an eagles talent in the
waste: I could have crept into any Aldermans
thumb-Ring: A plague off sighing and greese
it blowes a man vp like a bladder: there's
villanous newes abroad: heere was Sir Iohn
Braby from your father: you must goe to the
Court in the Morning: the same mad fellowe
off the North: Percy: And he off wales
that gaue Amamon the Bastinado: And made
Lucifer Cuckold: And swore the diuell his
true liedgman: vppon the Crosse off a
welsh hooke: what a plague call you
him,

Poyn: Owen, Glendower:

Fals: Owen. Owen: the same And his sonne in
lawe Mortimer: And old Northumberland
And the sprightly Scot off Scotts Dowglas
that runnes a horse-backe vpp a hill
perpendicular:

The toll book records, annually, the sale of horses at the fair. The description of each horse and the names of seller, buyer, and voucher were designed to prevent sale of stolen horses. The use of Latin to express dates and places is a carry-over from an earlier time when local records were written entirely in Latin. A single page is here shown.

The Fayre holden at markett Bosworth in the County of Leicester
for Sir Wolstan Dixie Knight apud festum Sancti petri 1623./.

William Alporte of Bitterscoate in the County of
Stafford yeoman bought a stoned whyte horse of
William Meade of Lutterworth in Comitatu of Leicester   } xiiij^s
yeoman trotting and Rackinge pryce
voucher Iohn Turner of Lutterworth predicto
yeoman.

Thomas Bannester of vpton in Comitatu Leicestrie
gentleman sould a graye Colte with a starre in
the heade trottinge to Thomas Bickers   } iij^l xvj^s viij^d
of South kilworth in Comitatu Leicestrie husbandman
pryce
voucher Lawrence vincent de vpton predicto.

Richard Ridgwaye of Ibstocke in the Comitatu
Leicestrie Carpenter sould a blacke mare with
a whyte in the heade trottinge to Richard   } xviij^s
Springthorpe of Leicester whittawer pryce
voucher Iohn Hues de ibstock predicto husbandman/

Hugh Marshall of Anstey in Comitatu Leicestrie sould
a Bay Colt stoned 2 yeares old trottinge
to walter Parsey of Swinsell in Comitatu   } iij^l iij^s iiij^d
Hunntington husbandman pryce
voucher Thomas Orme senior of Burbadge gentleman

Iohn Slater of Norborough in Comitatu Leicestrie husbandman
sould a whyte mare trotting with a headlesse
Cross vppon the Narr shoulder to Hughe   } xxxv^s viij^d
worthington of Hoppasse in Comitatu Staffordie husbandman
pryce
voucher Iohn Eames of Cadeby in Comitatu Leicestrie
husbandman

• • •

25 *Norborough*] *Narborough*, a town some eight   27 *Narr*] *near* or *left*.
or nine miles from Market Bosworth.

At the Fayre holden at markett Bosworth in the County of Leic
for Sr Wolstan Dixie knight apud festū Sti petri 1623

William Aleporte of Bitterswale in the County of
Staff yoman bought a stonde naggte horse of
william Ullradd of Lutterworth in Com of Leic   xviij s
yoman Brokinge and markinge prijse
voucher Iohn Edmonds of Lutterworth pdict
yoman

Thomas Wanmoster of upton in Com Leic
yont sould a graye Colte with a starr in
the fforhade Brokinge to Thomas Buckerds   iij li xxvj s viij d
of South Kilworth in Com Leic husband
prijse
voucher Lawrence Piment de upton pdict

Rychard Ridgwaye of Theston in the Com
Leic Carpentor sould a blacke mare with
a neppe in the fforhade Brokinge to Rychard   xxvij s
Symnge graye of Leicester nelthdwer prijse
voucher Iohn Lynde de ibstock pdict husb

Thomas Warren of Ansty in Com Leic sould
a Bay Colt stonde 2 yeards old Brokinge   iij li xiij s iiij d
to walter parby of Dunstead in Com
hunmington husb prijse
voucher Thomas Armeston of Warbadge gent

Iohn Slater of Narborowe in Com Leic husb
sould a neppe mare Brokinge with a hedastche   xxxv s viij d
Crosse upon the Nare sould to hnge
washington of Lyppaltc in Com Staff husb
prijse
voucher Iohn Lambe of Gadby in Com Leic
husb

Samuell Smith of walton in Com Leic   x d

PHILIP HOLLAND (PROBABLE WRITER)
THE CORONATION OF KING JAMES [CA. 1625]

Almost from its beginning, the italic hand challenged writers to develop beautiful hands. Calligraphy, the art of fine writing, though it did not originate with the italic hand, received a powerful stimulus from it. Many professionals and some talented amateurs achieved outstanding distinction in it. Among the amateurs two literary men attained some note as calligraphers: Roger Ascham (1515–1568) and John Davies of Hereford (1565–1618). The use of clubbed ascenders and descenders, like Holland's, became a vogue in the 1620's and 1630's. The description of the coronation is not here reproduced in its entirety.

The Coronation of King James and Queene Anne his wife 25 July 1603.

The Copie whereof was deliuered to his Matie by the Lo: Archbishop
of Canturbury who faythfully observed the forme sett downe in the
Ancient booke kept among the regalia at Westminster.

The Kinge and Queene come from Westminster bridge to the west
dore of the minster Church

They are receaued into the Church with an hymne or Anthem

They passe along through the body of the Church & soe vp to the Stage and
theare take theire places in theire severall seeges Royall

The King shewed to the people and they are required to make acknowledgment
of theire alleageance to his Matie by the Archbishop

which they doe by acclamations

The second Antheme is sung

The King and Queene descend from theire thrones & going to ye Altar
there offer the King: a pall and a pound of ye goulde the Q: likewise offereth

A prayer is sayde by the Archbishop

A sermon by the Bishop of Winchester

After the Sermon the King is moved by the Archb: to take his oath

The oath ministred by the Archbishop: and taken by the King

Then is sung come holy ghoste

A prayer by the Archbishop after that is donne

Letanie sayde or sung by the Bishop

Archbishop beginneth the Ceremonye of the anoynting wth the thankesgiuing
lift vp your harts &c:

After which the King coming to the Altar putteth of his vpper
garments

The author of "Vpon an houre glasse" is not known. The next piece, of which only a part is here shown, is by John Donne. The attractive and highly legible hand is typical of its time in the moderation of its ascenders and descenders. By 1630 most writers of the secretary hand were mixing in more italic forms than are to be seen here, the only examples being the last two letters of Autumnes (line 4) and the last three of Cinders (line 8). The punctuation is unusually heavy and unusually wanting in full stops.

Vpon an houre glasse:
Doe but consider this small dust
that runneth in the glasse
    by Autumnes mov'd
would you beleeve that it the body ere was   5
    of one that lov'd
Who in his Mistris flame playing like a Fly
    burnt to Cinders by her eye,
yes and in death as life vnblest
    to have it exprest   10
Even ashes of lovers finde no rest.

Marry: and love thy Flauia: for shee
hath all thinges wherewith others beauteous bee,
for though hir eyes be small, hir mouth is great,
though hir lipps Ivory, yet hir teeth are Iett,   15
though eyes ⟨they⟩ be dimme, yet she is light enough,
& though hir harsh haire fall, hir chinne is rough,
what though hir cheekes be yellow, hir head is red.
give hir thine, then shee has a mayden-head,
these thinges are beauties Elementes, where these   20
doe meete in one, that one must perfitt, please,
yf white & red, & each good quality
be in thy wench, nere aske where it doth ly;
In buying thinges perfum'd, wee aske yf there
be musk & amber in them, but not where;   25
though all hir partes be not ith vsuall place
she has an *Annagramm* of a good face;

• • •

4 *Autumnes*] Three other manuscripts agree in reading *atoms*, probably correctly. An atom was a mote or particle, here a grain of sand.

27 *Annagramm*] Both in MSS and in printed books, the italic hand or type was much used from the sixteenth to the eighteenth century for proper names, for foreign words (like this one), and for emphasis. The use of the italic hand here, then, does not constitute the kind of mixing mentioned in the head-note.

Upon an houre glasse:

Doe but consider this small dust
that runneth in the glasse
by Atumes mov'd
would you beleeve that it the body was
of one that lov'd
whoe in his Mts flame playing like a flye
burnt to Cinders by her eye.
Yet and in death as life unblest
to have 't exprest
then ashes of lovers finde no rest.

Rufus and loves thes Flauia: for shee
hath the things that goes with gentle beauteous bee
for though her eyes be small, her mouth is great,
though she her lippes Ibory. Yet her teeth are Iett,
though blacke be dimme. Yet she is light enough,
& though her harsh haire fall. Her skinne is rough,
what though her cheekes be yellow her head is red.
giue her then, she has a mayden-head.
these thinges are beauties elements, where they
be meete in one, that one must perfitt, pleas.
If white & red, & these good qualities
be in thy verses, sure then were it doeth les;
In buying thinges perfum'd, take after thy there
be muske & amber in them, but not there.
though all her partes be not its selfe alaw
yet has her Annagram of good her.
If wee could put the lettres but one way,
in that hard sorte, of woorde that could surseys.
when by the Gamutt some musicians make
a perfitt song, others will undertake
by the same Gamutt changed to equall it,
thinge that are simplye good, are none unfitt,
shee's faire as any, of her bee but her:
If none be, then is she singuler.

Most letters in this hand (not Jonson's own) are of the secretary form, but absence of long ascenders and descenders produces a general appearance quite foreign to the old secretary writing. Contractions and abbreviations are few. Final s is always secretary, but the others are consistently in one of two italic forms, the tall s made head first, not shaft first, and the short s much like ours. Of hs about half are italic, of rs somewhat less than half. The old-fashioned crossed ll makes only one or two appearances. The last part of the poem is not shown.

An Epigram vpon Inego Iones
to a freind./

Sir Inego doth feare it, as I heare,
   and labours to seeme worthie of that feare
That I should write vpon him some sharpe verse   5
   able to eate into his bones, and peirche
The marrowe, wretch, I quitt thee of thy paine
   th'art too ambitious and doost feare in vaine.
The Lybian Lyon huntes not butterflies,
   but makes the Cammell and dull asse his prize.   10
If thou art soe desireous to be read,
   seeke out some hungerie painter, that for bread
With rotten chalke, or cole vpon the wall
   can well designe thee to bee read of all
That sitt vpon the common draught or strand,   15
   thy forehead is too narrowe for my brand,
                         Ben: Ionson./

To Inego Marquesse would bee./

But cause thou hearest the mightie kinge of Spaine
   has made his Inego Marquesse, wouldst thou faine   20
Our Charles should make thee such? T'will not become
   All kings to doe the selfe same thinge with some,
Besides his man may Merritt it, and be
   A Noble, honest soule, whats this to thee?
Hee may haue skill and iudgment to designe   25
   Citties, and Temples, thou a Caue for wine
Or ale, hee build a Pallace, thou a shopp
   with sliding windowes and false lightes at topp./
Hee drawe a forum with Quadririll streetes,
   then paynt a layne, where thumbe the Pigmie meetes,   30

15 *draught*] *privy.*   *strand*] *channel* or *sewer.*
28 *lightes*] The final character might be mistaken for an italic *e;* it is the old contraction for *es;* see also *meetes,* line 30.
29 *Quadririll*] An error, doubtless through misreading of an unfamiliar word, for *quadrivial.*

An Epigram vpon Inego Jones
to a freind

Sᵣ Inego dose feare it, as I heard,
and Labours to seeme worthie of that feard
That I should write vpon him some sharpe verse
able to eate into his bones, and poetrey
The marrow, wretch, I quitt thee of thy paine
th'art too ambitious and doost feare in vaine.
The Lybian Lyon hunts not butterflies,
but makes the damett and dull asse his prize.
If thou art soe desirtous to be read,
seeke out some hungerie painter, that for bread
Wᵗ rotten chalke or coale vpon the wall
van will designd thee to bee read of all
That sitt vpon the comon draught or strand,
thy forehead is too narrowe for my brand,
                    Ben: Jonson.

To Inego Marquess would bie.

But cause thou hearest the mightie kinge of Spaine
hat made his Inego Marquess, wouldst thou faine
our Charles should make thee suche? t'will not become
All kings to doe the self same things wᵗ some,
Besides his man may Merritt it, and bie
A Noble, honest Soule, whats this to thee?
Hee may haue skill and iudgment to designe
Citties, and Temples, thou a shade for wine
or ale, hee build a Pallate, thou a shope
wᵗ sliding windowes and false ligte at tope.
Hee drawne a forum wᵗ Quadriuill streetes
Hin paynt a Legne, where thumbe the Pigmie meete,

Some whole words in this letter could easily have been written fifty years earlier than they were (Thrice, line 1; better, line 15; other, line 18), and the slashing descenders are more characteristic of 1580 than of 1630. Nevertheless the hand is a transitional one, containing some words that could have been written yesterday, and is easily recognizable *as belonging to the seventeenth century. Some little difficulty arises now and again from Napier's slovenly way of eliding an e with another letter, as in* departed *(line 8)* *and* offerd *(line 16); indeed it is possible that when he wrote* offerd *he thought he was writing* offered, *since he does not elsewhere leave such a letter out.*

Thrice honoured lady. It is not my vse, to be
troublesome to my mutch honoured frinds.
but when I am mutch importuned & that
by myne owne mynister, of whose lear
ning & preaching I and my, good neighbours 5
have had good experienc, I am Infourmed
that your last mynister mr Pen is very lately
departed out of this vale of misery. & by that
meanes, you are destitute of on that can
supply the place, these are therfore to in 10
treat this favour at your ladyships hands
that at my request you wilbe pleased to
admyt of mr Ruddle my minyster
into the vacant place, if you shall fynd
him better qualifyed for learning & preaching 15
then any other that happely may be offerd
vnto your choice, I doe heare that your ladyship
doth affect some other; but no way compara
ble for ought I can vnderstand with mr Rudle

• • •

12 *wilbe*] Out of context this would be read *wille,* but the context and Napier's habitual elisions make *wilbe* a safe reading here.

Mine honored Lady. It is not my use to be
troublesome to my much honored friend.
But when I am made importunate
by mine owne mynister, who shall have
many yeares my frend. And my good neighbour
have had good experience, I am informed
that of late mynister mr Don is very likely
to go out of this vale of misery. & by that
meanes, you are destitute of one that can
supply the place, this art thorow to m[?]
[?] this favour at yo[u]r Lordshipps hands
yt at my request you wille pleased to
admytt of mr Riddle my minister
into the vacant place, if you shall fynd
him better qualified for learning & living
then any others that apply, may be offred
vnto you therin, I doe assure yo[u]r Lordshipp
doe assure [?] other. But be very certaine
[?] for ought I co vnderstand wt mr Riddle
as you may easily fynd, iff it shall please
you to make tryall of him, I make no
doubt but mr Riddle will not only you
him selfe so serviceable, but also very thankfull
that yt shall gratefy him in this his suite.
And so if your Lordshipp will vouchsafe
him some favour in this first petition yt dir[?]
motiue to yo[u]r Lordshipp, I will cease to be more tro[u]
blesome vnto you & will ever rest

English from his first Servant
1631
Yo[u]r Ladishipps euer to be
co[m]manded Rich: Napier

45

SIR EDWARD HYDE
AUTOGRAPH LETTER
TO SIR MARMADUKE LANGDALE [1657]

Like the hand of Burghley's letter (Plate 25), Hyde's hand is difficult, and for the same general reason—haste and failure to form letters clearly. The resulting scrawl is at a few points impossible to make out with complete confidence. The hand is essentially

italic, but with a secretary residue in the letters c, d, e, g, p, and in some rs and final ss. Hyde, later Charles II's lord chancellor and earl of Clarendon, was the author of the famous History of the Rebellion.

I am to aske your pardon for hauinge two of yours upon my handes un-
answered, the one of the 2. the other of the 9: when the first came it
founde me in my bedd, vnable to write. and truly though I sate up
when the last came, I was not able to discharge that exercize, which
I hope you haue excused, for I am not naturally guilty of these
omissyons to my frends: I am confident I shall now see you shortly,
and wee shall then discource ouer our businesse at large, I do not differ
with you in my opinion of those persons you mencion, and exspecte
very little good from any of them; but from others who haue bene more
innocent I doe, and I am of opinion you will speedily see some dis-   10
order ther, that is, as soone as Crumwell hath complyed with the
desyres of his Parliament and assumed the title, which I belieue he hath
by this tyme done: All our stay heare is for mony, of which they
haue not helped us to one dollar, since our comminge hither, Don
Iohn returned the last night from Antwerpe. and this morninge the   15
kinge will speake with him, and then wee shall know what wee are
to trust to, in the meane tyme, wee owe for euery loafe we haue
eaten since our comminge ⟨hom⟩ hither; If it were otherwise Mr.
Barton should not haue bene this longe vnsupplyed, of which I
pray assure him, and that he shall heare effectually from me as   20
soone as is possible: I will trouble you ⟨f⟩ no farther at present, then
with the assurance that you shall always finde most heartily
                                        Sir

Bruxelles this
16. of May.
Sir Mar[maduke] Langdale:

your most affectionate
humble seruant   25
Edw: Hyde.

---

1 *yours*] Hyde's usual final *s* is curiously eccentric, with its superfluous upper loop.

3 *vnable*] An understanding of Hyde's usual final *e* can best be gained by examining a number of both his final and his medial *e*s; they are not essentially different.

5 *hope*] The *p* is the common secretary *p* but is made with an exaggerated attacking stroke; for more usual forms see the Pierrepoint letter, Plate 9.

17 *trust*] The main difficulty here is in the *r*, which cannot be duplicated in this letter. But the clue lies in the *r* of *ouer* (line 7), a perfect secretary *r* of a form very common two or

three decades earlier. In *trust* the first downstroke comes too far and thus produces what looks like an *x*; but the *x*s in lines 4, 5, and 8 are made with quite different pen movements.

19 *Barton*] It is impossible to determine whether this is *Burton* or *Barton*; the fact that the man quite possibly alluded to seems to have been *Barton* does not prove that Hyde wrote *Barton*.

21 *then*] This form of *than* was becoming obsolete in Hyde's time, and he may have thought he was writing *than*. But what he wrote looks like *then*.

116

I am to aske your pardon for haueing two of yours upon my handes un-
answered, the one of the 2. the other of the 9: when the first came it
founde me in my bed, vnable to write. and truly thought selfe very
when the last came, I was not able to discharge that exercize, which
I hope you haue excused, for I am not naturally guilty of those
auisstyout to my frends: I am confident I shall now see you shortly,
and wee shall then discourse ouer our businesse at larger, I do not differ
with you in my opinion of those persons you answerd, and expecte
very little good from any of them; but from others who haue beene more
innocent I doe, and I am of opinion you will speedily see some disorder here, that is, as soone as Cromwell hath complyed with the
dessyne of his parliant. and assured the title, which I beleeue he hath
by this tyme done: All one thy beare it for mony, of which they
haue not helped vs to our dollar, since our comminge hither, Doc-
tor he rehears the last night from Antwerp. and this morninge the
kinge will speake with him, and then wee shall know what wee are
to trust to, in the meane tyme, wee owe for euery loafe wee haue
eaten since our comminge hither; If it were otherwise Mr.
Barlow should not haue beene thus longe unsupplyed, of which I
pray assure him, and that he shall heare effectually from me as
soone as it possible: I will trouble you I no further at present, than
with the affeaunce that you shall alwayes finde mee heartily

your most affectionate
brother and frend

(Bruxells this
50 16. of May.

    8.

Sr Har. Lansdale:

William Lane uses both italic and secretary forms of lettering in this petition. To point out but a few: the ds, like most of the es, are in secretary; the rs and cs are secretary and italic; the ss, whether long or short, are italic. The long ascenders and descenders so characteristic of the secretary hand have gone, but abbreviation and contraction still abound. The general appearance of the hand is italic, but the secretary influence is still powerful.

To the Collective Body of the Kingdom of England.

False testimony (by God's owne verdict,) promerits both the Guylt, &
  punishment of those crymes, wherewith
it doth endeavour, to charge Innocency to Condemnation: And of that t'is
  the most vnnaturall, & indeed the
most pregnant which by silenc, vnder wrongefull sufferings, a man beare's
  against himselfe. As when the bold-faced
Imputations, of Popery, state-treason, Malignancy, disaffection, &c;
  do brow-beate the blushing   5
Modesty, of true Religion, fidelity, Country-zeale, selfe-defenc, &c;
  (able, where seconded with a
manly, (I need not say, a christian) resolution, to dastardize the power,
  & impudency, of death, & hell,) into an ex-
tasy of confession.
In prevention hereof, (despysing Family, estate, &c, all the endearements
  of this life,) when petitions could not prevayle, I en-
deavoured by flight to make some challeng to my Innocency; as yet not
  mann'd against the fury of all assaults, &   10
least willing to expire vnder the (mercyfull) sighes of Bondage: But at
  lenght tooke courage, when as
yet the enemys that persued me out of a pryvate splene, & for selfe-
  advantage, breathd forth threatnings, Imprysonments,
& Murther, to my very face, (the sacred vermin that are so engendred cannot
  possibly be preservd, but by the
putride matter of that corruption from whenc they did fyrst crawle,) to
  attempt a higher power (after 18 Moneths
sequestracion) to be admitted to my iust defenc.   15
wherevnto (with much reluctancy) I here gaind leave at ⟨last;⟩ lenght; &
  yet was persued with force, when I persued that leave: (Hy-
pocrisy must secure the guylt of so rich a prey:) Or else (as now), denyd
  the liberty of my proceedings, & by a sub-
tile Artifice, proiected into contempt, (for I must be cryminous,)
  (an Argument that this defenc (then exhibyted) is too
likely in the eye of a partiall Iudgment, to be left to a Committee-tryall,)
  I am enforcd at last, to prostrate it to the
veiwe, & common vote of my Country   20

• • •

2 *promerits*] The final *s* here and elsewhere does not appear to be intended as a contraction for *is* or *es;* Lane forms one of his two medial *ss* in the same way.

3 *the*] The squiggles after the last word are a space-filler.

13 *engendred*] The first *d* is written over a *g*.

To ye Collective Body of ye Kingdom of England.

Ffalse testimony (by God's owne verdict) p̃merits both y^e Guylt, & punishm^t of those crymes, whereon it doth endeavo^r to charge Innocency to Condemnation: And of y^e t'is y^e most unnaturall, & indeed those most pregnant wthly felons, under wrongefull sufferings, a man beares ag^t himselfe, as in y^e bed: faced Imputations, of Popery, state=treason, Malignancy, disaffection, &c, do beare: (evto those blushing Modesty, of true religion, fidelity, Country=zeale, selfe=defenc̄ &c; (able where founded wth a ... manly, (I need not say, a x̃ian) resolution, to dishonour of pow̃, & impudency, of death, & hell,) into an ... tary of confession.

In p̃vention hereof, (despysing shame, estate, & all y^e endearem^{ts} of y^e life,) my petitions could not p̃vaile, y^e en= devoured by flight to make some challeng to my Innocency; as yet not maim'd ag^t y^e fury of assaults, & least willing to expire under the (mercyfull) sighes of bondage: But at length tooke courage; whenas y^e enemys y^t issued me out of a private sphere, & for selfe=advantage, breath'd forth threatnings, Imprisonm^t, & Murther, to my very face, (the secred vermin y^t are so engendred cannot possibly be s̃found, but by the putride matter of y^e corruption for whome they did first crawle,) to attempt a higher pow̃ (aft^r 12 Months sequestration) to be admitted to my just defence.

whereunto (wth much voluntary) I have gain'd leave at length, & yet was p̃sued in force, in I p̃sued y^e leave, (Hy= pocrisy must forme y^e guylt of so with a prey:) Or else (as now) deny'd y^e liberty of my p̃ceedings, & by a sub= tile Artifice pierced into contempt, (for I must be crymin̄ous,) (an arguem^t of this detested casuistry (as its too likely,) in y^e eye of a p̃tiall judgm^t, to be left to a Com̃ittee=tryall,) I am enforced at last, to p̃trochle to the voice, & com̃on vote of my Country.

To you therefore (for whom I suffer in y^e defenc̄ of o^r com̃on rights, invaded on all sydes under y^e shew of y^e res= titution) thus compelled, (& what otherwise can I doe) depriv'd all meanes of livelyhood, & altogether con= straind to wander in y^e Maze & whimseys of an unconstrain'd jurisdiction. To I tender this defence, wherein, if I shall appeare guylty, of any scandall or treachery to y^e Church, or state, (tempted thereunto wth no sparing importunity, & too much reward;) or of any violenc̄ ag^t, or neglect to, my Neighbo^{rs} welfare, (though plundered on both sydes to considerable & frequent losses,) I desire with my life (too unworthy in my owne esteeme, might it be a thousand tymes sacrific'd,) to expiate those offences.

But if y^e sons of Belialt (& in wch also you may take a view of y^e p̃fort̃ to formatio: for wee cannot beleeve y^t knaves, Ignaroes, & selfe=seekers, can at once what be formed, by y^e plastique pow̃ of a gt̃ Testimoniall, or of a privy vote, into Godly, learned, & Orthodox Divines,) who have gone in y^e way of Cain, & run'd greedily after y^e error of Balaam for reward;) have risen up ag^t mee; I do here (once for all) charge you, in y^e name of God & ye oppressed Brethren, that you do unto ye Cppwr̃ as must not pitty,) as they have deserved.

So shall you (& you cannot otherwise,) put away ye evill fro ye selves; (you will be p̃tys in those filns, or stakes in my sufferings;) & those wch remaine shall heare, & feare, & shall henceforth com̃it no more any evill among you. Deut 19. 16. to ye end.

Y^r wholy devoted to ye service of
God & his Country.

From my exile.
1647:

W: L:

47A

J. DE BEAU CHESNE AND J. BAILDON
A NEW BOOKE, CONTAINING ALL SORTS OF HANDS

[1611]

The two hands shown here are examples of court hand, the term applied primarily to the hands of the superior courts of law. Even though differences arose between the hands of the different courts, court hands *always had much in common: the majority of the letters are formed in the same way; they are upright and regular; and they tend to be distinct from one another.*

The faste hande in the Common Place.

Robertus hampton & Thomas Gunston Armigeri in proprijs personis suis
     petunt versus

hugonem Sampson Armigerum manorem de Morgrave cum pertinenciis in
     marcham

hemsbye vt ius et hereditatem suam & in quod idem hugo non habet ingressum

nisi post disseisinam quam Robertus habuit inde iniusce & sine iudicio etsetera   5

3 *Armigerum*] The *g* lacks the lower loop, probably through the engraver's carelessness.   4 *et*] The *t* is also defective lacking its top.

47B

MARTIN BILLINGSLEY
THE PENS EXCELLENCIE   [1618]

It will be seen in the alphabet that no distinction is made between a capital and a minuscule in the letters h, k, and l.

[Chancery hand]

Iacobus dei gracia Anglie Scocie Francie & hibernie
Rex fidei defensor etcetera Vicecomiti London salutem. Tibi
precipimus quod attachias Philippum Iohnson Armigerum Ita
quod eum habeas coram nobis in Cancellaria nostra in etcetera

A. a. a. B. b. b. C. c. cc. D. d. d'. E. e. ee. F'. f. f.   5
G. g. g'. h. h. h. I. i. ij. k. k. k'. l. ll'. l. M. m. mm.
N. n. n. O. o. oo. P. pre. pp. Q. que. q. R. r. r. r. R. S. s.   ·
s'. st. T. t. tt. v. u. v. u. u. w. w. x. x. y. y. z. z. &. us.

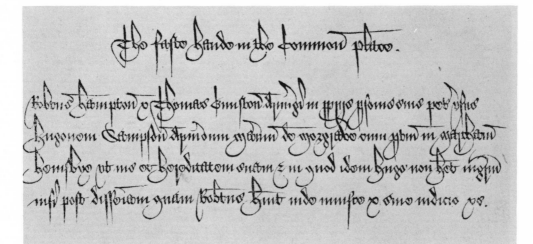

48 COURT ROLL OF THE MANOR OF HURSTMONCEUX, SUSSEX   1530

A clear, neatly written example of a legal hand. Two of the marginal notes are in a secretary hand. Only the first portion of the document is shown.

herstmonnceux

Essonia

Curia tenta ibidem vltimo die Septembris Anno regni Regis henrici Octaui vicesimo secundo

nulla

ad istam Curiam venerunt Eustachius Braham armiger Tenens terre nuper Willelmi Cheyney Tenens viij^d

terre nuper Thome Dygby militis de Gate Tenens viij^d

Fines

terre nuper Ricardi Sakevyle Willelmus a Wodde Ricardus Shepard et Oliuerus Trodes qui dant domino de viij^d

fine pro secta Curie relaxata per annum prout patet super

eorum capita etcetera

homagium ibidem presentat quod Iohannes hantowne et anna uxor eius qui de domino nuper tenuerunt   5

vnum Tenementum vnum gardinum et viginti acras terre natiue cum pertinenciis

heriettum vj^s viij^d

vocat' hogebaynys scituat' et iacen' in parochia de herstmonnceux vnde reddiderunt per annum

domino xx^s et heriettum ipsius Iohannis qui quidem Iohannes iam

mortuus est post cuius mortem accidit domino nomine herietti vj^s viij^d de extenta Et sic eadem

anna inde remanet tenent' pro termino vite sue

etcetera   10

Thomas a Stocke   Item presentat quod agnes a Stok qui de domino nuper tenuit certam terram vocatam Elyottes per

redditum per annum xij^s et certam terram natiuam vocatam Wedottes per redditum

heriettum

per annum xij^s et aliam terram vocatam Breggers per redditum per annum xxiij^d obijt inde seisita per

Cuius mortem accidit domino de herietto vnum bouem Et quod

Thomas a Stok est eius filius maxime Iuuenis et proximus heres et plene etatis Et modo predictus

Thomas venit et presens in Curia petit admitti ad terras

releuium xxiiij^s predictas cum pertinenciis Et super hoc Dominus concessit predictas terras cum pertinenciis prefato

Thome habend' et tenend' sibi et heredibus suis ad voluntatem domini secundum consuetudinem

manerij

. . .

4 *armiger*] The writer uses three kinds of minuscule *a*; cf. *Braham* (line 4) and the initial *a* in *aliam* (line 12).
5 *qui*] The mark of abbreviation above the final *i* is meaningless; cf. *viginti* (line 7).
8 *vocat'*] On the use of the apostrophe instead of an ending see Introduction, page 22).
11 *Stocke Item*] The *ke* is written over the *It'*.

49

PHILIP HOBY
BOND OR NOTE OF HAND 1541

This, another example of the legal hand of this period, is clear and regular in contrast to Hoby's signature. The seal has long since disappeared.

Thys byll made the xxvjth day off Februarie yn the xxxijth yere of the
reyng of our souerayng lord kyng Henry the eight, Witnessyth that I
Phelyp Hobye Esquyer haue borowyd and receauyd the day of the
makyng of thes presentes of sir George Lanzon knyght the Somme of
twentye powndes sterlyng The which somme of xx^{li} sterling I the   5
seyd Phelip Hobye do bynde my selffe by thes presentes my heires &
executors to recontente & paye to the seid sir Geoge Lanzon his
executors or assignez before or at the Feast of Easter next comyng
after the date hereof In Witnes wherof I the seid Phelyp hobye
to this byll ⟨hah⟩ haue setto my seale and subscribed my name   10
the day and yere abouewreten

                    per me phelyp hoby

This byll made the xxvj day off ffebruario yn the xxxj yere of the
reyng of o[ur] souerayng lord kyng henry the eyght. witnessyth that I
Rychard Robyns ffysmer wzne bejeckyd o rewaryd the day of the
makyng of thes p[rese]nt of R Roye Lanzow bought the some of
xxvj pownde styrlong. the whych some of xxvj li ffi I the
seyd Rychard Robyns do bynd my selfe by thes p[rese]nt my ffull
exentres to p[er]contente o polye to the seyd R Roye Lanzow his
exentors or Assignes bothe or of At the ffest off Ester next comyng
After the date thereof In witnes wherof I the seid Rychard Robyns
to this byll hath hthno otto my seale o subscribed my name
the Ay o yere Abonelopeten

Be me Rychard Robys

50

NICHOLAS KYNNERSLEY

AUTOGRAPH LETTER TO ELIZABETH,

COUNTESS OF SHREWSBURY 1588

The letter was written by a henchman of the countess' at a time when she and her husband, "me lord," were at variance with one another. It is in a legal hand—the hand with which Kynnersley was probably most familiar in his professional duties. The signature, written at the bottom of the page, is not reproduced.

This nyght after Iohn was gone with me later ezabell told me that gylbard

Dyckensson came to hur in the bachowsse & axed yff your honor were here

      & she

answared no & he axed when you went aweay & sed yesterday he axed when

you wold come agyne she answared shortly as she thowght. & lat at nyght

there came a boye from sheffeld in a grene cote & talked with them in

      the stable   5

& sed he moste goe very yerly in the mornyng to sheffeld agyn what ys

      his meanyng

be thes questyons & the lacky comyng so late & goyng so yerly in the mornyng

I knowe not except yt be to bryng me lo[rd] worde off your absence here &

      so that he

myght com vppon the soden & fynd you aweay so I leve yt to your honors

      wysdom

to conseder off yt as you thynke beste bot I thynke good you were here. mr   10

knyveton ryd by to day to sheffeld as I was told & called not as I was

told which I marvell off. me. lady arbella at viij off the clocke this nyght was

mery & eates hur meat well bot she went not to the stolle this vj days therefore

I wold be glad off your ladyships comyng yff there were no oyer matter bot

      that so I

beseke the allmyghty preserue your ladyship in helthe & send you sonne

      a good &   15

comfordable end off all your great trobles & g[r]effes Wynffeld this Twysday

the v off novembar at viij off the clocke at nyght 1588

                  your .ho. moste dewtyfull bound

                  obedyent sarvand

---

1 *gone*] There is an extra minim in this word.
5 *grene*] There is an extra minim in this word.
12 *lady arbella*] Lady Arabella Stewart, a grand-daughter of the countess of Shrewsbury.
14 *oyer*] other; common usage allowed *y* for *th* only initially.

ye novembay at viij A ꝰ clocke at night 1563

yo. to ye moste bownd ffrind

Robert Sebauin

BOOKS RECOMMENDED FOR READING AND REFERENCE

CHARLES JOHNSON AND HILARY JENKINSON. *English Court Hand A.D. 1066 to 1500.*
Illustrated from the Public Records. 2 vols. Oxford: Clarendon Press, 1915.
> An indispensable work containing many plates and transcripts and pro-
> viding illustrated discussions of the letters and symbols found in medieval
> manuscripts, many of them common in the sixteenth century.

HILARY JENKINSON. *The Later Court Hands in England from the Fifteenth to the
Seventeenth Century.* 2 vols. Cambridge University Press, 1927.
> A companion work to the foregoing and, with its numerous plates and
> transcripts, the most thorough reference work on the handwritings of the
> centuries covered. It discusses other hands in addition to the court hands—
> text hands, secretary, and italic hands.

L. C. HECTOR. *The Handwriting of English Documents.* London: E. Arnold
[1958].
> A concise guide, with plates and transcripts illustrating a great variety of
> hands from A.D. 700 to 1830. One chapter is devoted to abbreviation and
> contraction.

NOËL DENHOLM-YOUNG. *Handwriting in England and Wales.* Cardiff: University
of Wales Press, 1954.
> Valuable mainly for its historical matter. The reproductions are of poor
> quality, and few are transcribed.

MURIEL ST. CLARE BYRNE. "Elizabethan Handwriting for Beginners," *Review of
English Studies,* I (1925), 198–209.
> One of the earliest recognitions of the need on the part of research students
> of sixteenth-century literature to study its handwriting systematically.

SAMUEL A. TANNENBAUM. *The Handwriting of the Renaissance.* New York:
Columbia University Press, 1930.
> The first full-scale attempt to describe, discuss, and illustrate the secretary

handwriting. Brings together much information not easily to be found elsewhere but is not always reliable.

BERTHOLD LOUIS ULLMAN. *The Origin and Development of Humanistic Script.* Rome: Edizioni di Storia e Letteratura, 1960.

A detailed and illustrated account of the hand that was the chief progenitor of the italic hand.

ALFRED FAIRBANK AND BRUCE DICKINS. *The Italic Hand in Tudor Cambridge.* Cambridge Bibliographical Society Monograph No. 5. 1962.

Cambridge was an early and important center of the italic writing in England. The book contains excellent plates.

ANDREW WRIGHT. *Court-Hand Restored.* London, Stevens and Sons, Ltd, 1912.

Though first published in 1776, still valuable for its illustrations of many court and business hands and its lists of abbreviations.

R. E. LATHAM. *Revised Medieval Latin Word-List from British and Irish Sources.* London: Oxford University Press, 1965

A glossary of words and meanings peculiar to Medieval Latin, with the earliest and latest recorded dates for each.

CHARLES TRICE MARTIN. *The Record Interpreter: a Collection of Abbreviations, Latin Words and Names Used in English Historical Manuscripts and Records* (3rd impression). London: Stevens and Sons, Ltd. [1949].

ADRIANO CAPPELLI. *Lexicon Abbreviaturarum. Dizionario di Abbreviature Latine ed Italiane usate nelle Carte e Codici Specialmente del Medio-Evo.* Sixth edition. Milan: U. Hoepli, 1961.

CHRISTOPHER R. CHENEY. *Handbook of Dates for Students of English History.* London: Royal Historical Society, 1961.

Valuable for determining dates of documents dated by regnal years, saints' days, and so forth.

FREDERICK M. POWICKE AND E. B. FRYDE. *Handbook of British Chronology* (2nd ed.). London: Royal Historical Society, 1961.

Contains many useful lists, with dates, of English kings, bishops, and other officers and a chapter on various methods of reckoning time.

WALTER WILSON GREG. *English Literary Autographs, 1550–1650.* 3 vols. London: Oxford University Press, 1932.

The hundreds of specimens of handwriting by dramatists, poets, and prose writers, with transcripts, provide abundant and varied material for practice in reading.

HILDA E. P. GRIEVE. *Some Examples of English Handwriting.* Chelmsford, England: Essex Record Office Publications, No. 6, 1949.

———— *More Examples of English Handwriting.* Essex Record Office Publications, No. 9, 1950.

———— *Examples of English Handwriting.* Essex Record Office Publications, No. 21, 1954.

These pamphlets contain many reproduced specimens of renaissance hands, with transcripts, and are inexpensive and easily obtainable from the Essex Record Office.